# FIND YOUR CLEAR VISION

# FIND YOUR CLEAR VISION

A New Mindset to Create a

Vibrant Personal or Professional

Brand with Purpose

LISA GUILLOT

COPYRIGHT © 2023 LISA GUILLOT

All rights reserved.

FIND YOUR CLEAR VISION
*A New Mindset to Create a Vibrant Personal or Professional Brand with Purpose*

ISBN   978-1-5445-3641-5  *Hardcover*
         978-1-5445-3640-8  *Paperback*
         978-1-5445-3639-2  *Ebook*

# CONTENTS

Introduction   ix

**1**
Creativity   3

**2**
Feminine and Masculine Energy   23

**3**
Move from Breakdown to Breakthrough   37

**4**
Identifying Your Paradox Pattern   53

**5**
Meet Your Paradox Pattern   63

## 6
Build Your Clear Vision   89

## 7
Create and Expand Your Energy   149

## 8
Trust Your New Identity   189

## 9
Choose Flow on Purpose   209

## 10
Your Outer Platform   223

## 11
Positioning   239

## 12
Messaging and Visual Content   281

Conclusion   305

Acknowledgments   309

*To my visionary family.
You are my light.*

# INTRODUCTION

YOU'RE READY FOR CHANGE, YOU WANT TO CHANGE. You've tried too.

You went the traditional route and found a mentor and hired a coach to tell you who to be and what to do. You tried talk therapy, light therapy, and that reiki master your friend recommended. You've signed up for countless online courses to find your purpose, build your career, or reconnect to your inner wisdom.

But nothing sticks, and you find yourself going back to the same pattern of knowing something's missing but not knowing what to do next. Your pattern has you stuck in a loop of exhaustion, thinking, "Oh no! Is this all there is? If so, this sucks."

I know what's missing.

You want to stand out but don't feel safe being you—deeply, truly, and without apology—so instead, you show up as what you think a professional should be, but it doesn't vibe with you.

## INTRODUCTION

Imposter syndrome kicks in and you double down on the thought, "This is who I need to be to get to the next level in my life." And you try harder, working longer hours, trying to prove that you should be something more than you are, anchoring into a pattern that becomes so woven into your daily routine that it feels natural.

Until something inside of you softly whispers, "All this running around in circles is making me dizzy."

Or your body starts to shut down on you, and you miss your train stop because you've slept through it. Again. Or you get home just in time to put the kids to bed, but you are so on edge that they feel your anxiety and look at you with confusion. They don't even recognize you.

You don't recognize yourself.

It's time. Time to stop wanting to change, and time to commit to it. Do you feel the difference between wanting something and committing to it? Wanting something puts it out in the distance, somewhere you can only dream of, something that other people have, but you don't. And you can list all the reasons why you don't have it.

You don't have the time, the energy, or a roadmap.

You don't trust yourself. You've tried to change, but you keep coming back to the same ol' same ol'.

## FIND YOUR CLEAR VISION

It's time to commit. Committing to something puts your foot on the road. Even if you don't know where the road leads, you are willing to be on the road to somewhere. And somewhere is better than where you are.

When you commit to taking the first step, you'll start to notice a lightness. Your energy starts to pop because you have a little more wiggle room for yourself, a little extra space to take a deep breath and exhale and think, "I want to do it differently this time."

If you aren't willing to commit to being on the road with me, to dropping the excuses, rumination, and procrastination—put this book down, it's not for you.

If you are willing to explore, get creative and messy, not knowing the outcome, but trusting yourself in the process, welcome. Welcome to the Messy Middle. You're ready to find your Clear Vision.

Your Messy Middle is the space between who you were and who you are becoming. In order to move from the past into the future, through the Messy Middle, it's time to build your Inner Platform. In marketing terms, a "platform" is the framework to connect your business to your audience. Your Inner Platform is the framework to connect who you were to who you are becoming. It's a 360-degree view of how you see and believe in yourself. It's built with a creative mindset plus self-awareness, inner trust, and elevated energy. When

## INTRODUCTION

your Inner Platform is rock solid, you become a magnet for opportunity.

It's time to stop fighting for your limitations. Reinvention doesn't exist in how you've done it in the past. Your past will have you running on empty, going in circles, and getting nothing done.

When you build your Inner Platform, you are committing to trusting yourself. Trusting who you are leads to massive changes in your decision-making, and naturally, you become someone whom others can trust.

When you build your Inner Platform, you are committing to expanding your energy. When your energy is nurtured, nourished, and never-ending, you can be with the ups and downs of life because you are supported by your personal habits and rituals.

When you build your Inner Platform, you are committing to becoming more self-aware. When you do the mindset work to clarify who you are, what your purpose is here on earth, and the legacy you are meant to leave behind, you become the confident creator of your life and become known for your authentic voice and message.

When you build your Inner Platform, you are committing to finding your Clear Vision. When you clarify your vision and why it's important to you, you become a visionary. Your confidence is seen, felt, and remembered. That is your legacy, that is your life by design.

## FIND YOUR CLEAR VISION

Building your Inner Platform is how personal and professional brands are built from the inside out. It's a sustainable way to create your life by design. For so long professionals have been handed down a list of implied rules that you are unwilling to follow. Transformation does not exist in the past; it's reinvented from a deep sense of inner trust, personal energy, and your Clear Vision.

I've seen this transformation hundreds of times. My clients have transformed their lives, businesses, and careers following this exact framework. And it's possible for you to do so too. Just commit to the process. Commit to being in the Messy Middle, and I'll be your creative guide to help you reinvent who you are and unlock a Clear Vision of your life and career.

Will it be easy? Probably not. Will it be fun? Sometimes. Will you see, feel, and be a different person at the end of the book? Yes, absolutely—if you trust yourself and do it.

The world is waiting for you to shine bright.

## MY REINVENTION

I had to lose my eyesight in order to see myself.

I was constantly striving to be perfect at everything—the perfect business owner, designer, wife, mother, stepmother. It left me quarantined in the hospital with a life-altering case of shingles the day my daughter was born.

## INTRODUCTION

I thought shingles were something old people got. Not me, a 30-something woman. But I was wrong. Shingles is the result of a weakened immune system, and for me it was stress.

Let me step back a few years. In 2009 I was laid off from Paper Source, a stationery and gift retailer based in Chicago, where I was the senior design manager for their catalog and website. 2008–2009 was a rough patch for creatives. When the economy hits a snag, advertising and design are often the first to be let go. It wasn't the first time I was laid off; I was also let go after September 11th, so I knew the drill. Layoffs always seem to happen on Friday mornings. This time around, instead of applying for unemployment, I started my branding studio, Step Brightly. I started creating full branding suites—websites, logos, style guides, advertising, and print materials for lifestyle brands, small businesses, and retail shops.

A few months later I got married and became a stepmom.

I didn't know how to be a mom to two rambunctious boys, so I compared myself to other "perfect" moms who seemed to have it all together with snack packs of Cheerios and extra clothes in a Ziploc baggie "just in case." I judged moms whose minivans smelled like wet diapers, and I judged myself for not knowing how to change a diaper. I knew who I didn't want to be—someone who couldn't hold it all together, someone who didn't know what she was doing, but I didn't know who I was.

Fast forward to 2013, when my husband and I had our first baby who was now a rambunctious little boy who loved to

## FIND YOUR CLEAR VISION

roughhouse with his big brothers. I was making more money than I ever had before in my business. I was on the board of directors of AIGA Chicago, the Professional Association for Design. By all accounts, it looked like I was thriving in life and business.

The overachieving perfectionist in me—the same one who could find a typographical error on a page in a heartbeat and see that a neutral gray had too much blue in it—was trying to bring that high level of perfection right into life, work, and momming.

Get this. I wanted to have a second child, so, as any overachieving marketing exec would do, I pitched the idea to my husband, in a PowerPoint presentation. I calculated the loads of laundry we do each week, how much we drive, shop, and all the other to-do's that would be required to add another human into the mix, and, the award-winning concept behind the presentation was "Don't worry, honey! I've got it all completely handled!"

I felt the mounting pressure of motherhood, and, being a businesswoman, I felt disconnected from myself. So, what did I do? I added more things to my to-do list. I started an entrepreneurial creative community for women in Chicago with two friends, a writer and photographer. Deep down I feared I would become that overweight mom in yoga pants, with two kids stuck in the suburbs. I refused to let my perfect businesswoman persona be scarred by a minivan with goldfish crumbled on the floor.

## INTRODUCTION

What's God's gift to overachieving perfectionists who are always on time? A scheduled C-section.

I knew the exact time our second baby was arriving. But when I awoke from the daze of the epidural, I was quarantined in the left wing of the hospital. The doctors and nurses wore protective gear when they entered my room to tell me I couldn't hold my newborn because they didn't know what was swelling on the side of my face. The left side of my face—my eye, nose, and lips—had swollen to the size of a baseball and was electric red.

I was crushed.

I could only see my baby out of one eye. I couldn't hold her or take care of her. I couldn't do what I do best: take responsibility for all the things—to prove I can do it all.

I was hiding under a pattern of behaviors and stories of who I thought I should be: perfect, wildly creative, professional, lovable, and good enough. So, to live in a world with this constant narrative of not being good enough, I overcompensated with a thin veil of perfection to hide my not-enoughness.

What got me into this mess?

Cultural, societal, and generational messages—told to us through the media, shared in stories, and written into our daily lives—have us believe that women should "have it all" but do it in a world that is not set up to support us. Women spend a

# FIND YOUR CLEAR VISION

lot of time and energy proving they are capable of "having it all" when "it all" is rarely defined. This repetitive paradoxical pattern leads to stress, insomnia, missed periods, massive headaches, autoimmune disorders, and, for me, recurring shingles. And it's not acceptable.

A Paradox Pattern is a repeatable pattern embedded into your thoughts, actions, and behaviors used to prove that you are capable, lovable, and enough to have it all. The paradox is… you are already enough.

My Paradox Pattern is called The Polished Perfectionist. The Polished Perfectionists' greatest fear is that someone will think we are weak. Actively, out in the world, this pattern shows up as rumination, overcompensation, and constant polishing of distracting, yet shiny objects. Passively, inside my head, perfectionism shows up as imposter syndrome and a complete lack of vulnerability, since vulnerability, at least in my mind, was perceived as a sign of weakness.

It took a team of doctors, two master life coaches, and a Buddhist monk to help me see who I was without my Paradox Pattern, and to see the false identity I had created to hide who I really was.

Some authors kick off Chapter 1 with the breakdown of all breakdowns. And you would think that I would have learned my lesson—that the baseball-sized swelling on my face and a Rudolph-red nose would have been a sign, but it wasn't. Not yet.

## INTRODUCTION

My pattern was woven so deeply that I created my life to operate in full-blown stress mode. And the worst thing about it was that I had no idea. I thought this identity was "normal."

Here's the thing about your Paradox Pattern—it doesn't work. It won't leave you feeling what you most desire—to be loved, validated, respected, fulfilled, or enough.

I thought if I built my business on my own and didn't ask for help then I'd prove I was capable.

If I did it perfectly, then I would be validated.

If I created award-winning work, then I would be respected.

If I lowered my expectations or slowed down, then I would fail.

I was really busy creating a world where my fears wouldn't come true.

I kept trying harder, working longer, and pushing myself to the point that my body said, "No more!" And I broke.

I'm curious if you ever noticed that for yourself. That when you push,

or provoke,

or fix,

## FIND YOUR CLEAR VISION

or pretend,

or hide,

or yell,

or patronize,

or blame,

you break.

The best thing about a breakdown? It can also be a break*through*.

Even though my world was a mess of kids, pregnancy, and entrepreneurship, I was still running my brand strategy studio, and successfully.

Since I graduated from the University of San Francisco and the Academy of Art University, I've been in the creative industry. I helped clients brainstorm and create brand identity programs. A brand identity program is the look and feel of the brand. It's the image that's left in the customer's mind when the brand touches them.

A brand identity shows up in visuals like patterns, colors, and typography. It also includes messaging and taglines. Ultimately all of these pieces come together to create the website, print materials, and social media messaging and

## INTRODUCTION

graphics. When it all works together seamlessly, you have an award-winning brand identity.

With a consistent message and lots of advertising dollars, a company will gain brand awareness and loyalty from its customers. When I say "Nike," you think, "Just do it." When I say "McDonald's," you think, "I'm loving it." Like I said, with lots of advertising dollars, American brands seep into our subconscious pretty effectively.

Human beings also have identities. Looking in a mirror has you thinking what you see is what you get, but we know that isn't true, because perceptions can be deceiving. The most put-together person in a room could be having a conversation in their head that is full of second-guessing and shame.

A personal or professional brand, when built from an identity of who we think we should be—often masked with half-truths, and stylistically covered in overwhelm, shame, or perfection—rubs us the wrong way. As an outsider, we can't put our finger on it, but we sense a disconnection between the human and the façade they are presenting.

Here's why: personal and professional branding is an exchange of energy. Branding is the feeling you leave with others. Your personal and professional brand is the stories, memories, and emotions of your presence. The problem is

## FIND YOUR CLEAR VISION

that many people start building their brand from what they see in a mirror, reflecting back an illusion of who they *think* they are instead of who they want to become.

In Lewis Carroll's *Alice in Wonderland,* Alice is trying to find her way out of the dream-like, upside-down world. She stumbles across the blue caterpillar smoking a hookah who asks,

*"Who are you?"*

She replies, *"I hardly know sir, just at present, at least I know who I was when I got up this morning, but I think I must have changed several times since then."*

*"What do you mean by that? Explain yourself,"* the caterpillar says.

*"I can't explain myself, I'm afraid, sir, because I'm not myself you see. I'm afraid I can't put it more clearly, for I can't understand it myself to begin with, and being so many different sizes in a day is very confusing."*

When the world is a kaleidoscope of differing sizes, shapes, and colors, and you don't know which way is up, who are you? How do you shed your Paradox Pattern to show up as who you really are?

You build an Inner Platform. Here's how.

## INTRODUCTION

Your Inner Platform is the foundational mindset needed to build a successful personal or professional brand; one that resonates, makes an impact, and is truly authentic because it is you without the false narrative of who you think you should be. Your Inner Platform raises you out of the dropbox of your repetitive Paradox Pattern and into a life where you are fully expressed and feel safe being you.

## FOUR INGREDIENTS OF YOUR INNER PLATFORM

### Clear Vision

Creating a Clear Vision of your future is the first step to reinventing your life without the constraints of your Paradox Pattern. When you have a Clear Vision, you become a visionary.

### Inner Trust

When you trust yourself, there is no room for second-guessing. Decisions become clear and you become trustworthy. Inner trust leads to confidence, influence, and authority.

### Self-Awareness

Building a relationship with our most vibrant self and embodying self-awareness leads to your authentic voice and message. When you are self-aware, you no longer take things personally.

**FIND YOUR CLEAR VISION**

## Expanded Energy

Expanding your energy allows you to laser focus. When you have more energy, you have the mental capacity to imagine and create more ideas, creativity, and impact.

Remember the Buddhist monk from my shingles story? Oh yeah, and remember how I didn't learn my lesson the first, second, or third time? Three years passed before I began to attend a meditation ceremony at the local Buddhist temple in Oak Park, Illinois, on Fridays at 11 am. I needed some type of peace and quiet in my life in between potty training and building brands.

I put the 11 am public meditation time as a recurring event on my calendar. It was a really big deal for me to have something for myself on the calendar. My calendar was filled to the brim with things for other people. This was the first time I had anything on it just for myself.

I was sitting crisscross applesauce on a thin mat that morning, breathing in silence with a few other people who were also meditating, when I began to notice something. I had enough space in between my breaths where I could hear my thoughts. They weren't talking to me. They were just waiting for me to catch up to them. To notice and to play with them. To bounce them from side to side.

I started to tingle like my skin was being touched by tiny dots of light. I turned my palms upward, so they were facing the

## INTRODUCTION

sky. I felt the lightweight air resting on my palms. I felt the energetic pull of my thoughts introducing themselves. And they were fun and playful and creative. I could feel myself being me. A new pattern started to emerge that day, a reinvention of who I was becoming, and it was delightful.

I knew who I would be without my Paradox. Me.

## WHAT THIS BOOK WILL TEACH YOU

Nowhere else will you find a book that transforms your mindset and gives you the strategy to build your personal or professional brand. Those are typically two books—a personal development book and a business strategy book. Here, you get both. I'm bringing 20+ years of brand strategy expertise and creative mindset to you to help you find your Clear Vision, build your Inner Platform, and share it with the world. In this book, I will teach you:

- How to release the limiting beliefs and paradoxical patterns that have you stuck

- How to build your Inner Platform to create inner trust, expanded energy, and self-awareness

- How to sit with uncomfortable triggers in your personal and professional life and have the tools to move forward with confidence

## FIND YOUR CLEAR VISION

- How to have agency over your decision-making

- How to feel safe being seen for who you are

- How to create your Clear Vision using the creative process, because, yep, you are creative—everyone is

- What a personal and professional brand looks like when it's built from who you really are

- A roadmap of how to show up as a visionary in your personal or professional brand

- What your Visionary Values are and how to share them on social media

- The six must-haves in your personal or professional brand to stand out

## WHAT THIS BOOK WILL *NOT* TEACH YOU

Any book that tells you they have all the answers is wrong, especially when it comes to building a personal or professional brand. Building a brand from a cookie-cutter strategy is a surefire way to show up just like everyone else.

Those types of books don't have the answers—you do. Trying to find your "why" has you looking in the past, and we are

## INTRODUCTION

building your future. Only you know yourself. You are the heart, soul, and visionary leader of your reinvention, and it starts on the inside. This book is the roadmap to release, rebuild, and renew the confidence and conviction of who you are meant to be in the world.

## WHY ME

My name is Lisa Guillot, and I live my life from my Clear Vision to help others find theirs.

The first company I worked for out of college was called Addis, the Brand Essence Company. We worked with companies like Pottery Barn Kids, Sephora, and The Gap. Now I help extraordinary people, like you, find their essence and future vision.

I've spent time in creative design studios, ad agencies, and marketing departments, bringing ideas to life using the creative process. Now I've taken that framework and lead my clients through their own creative process.

I'm an entrepreneur at heart. After being let go twice, I started my branding studio, Step Brightly, in 2009 and my coaching practice, Be Bright Lisa, in 2016.

I'm a branding expert. I'm a professionally certified transformational life and leadership coach. My clients include senior-level executives at Fortune 500 media and entertainment companies, and in marketing, financial services, law, and

**FIND YOUR CLEAR VISION**

tech. My clients also include ambitious entrepreneurs in the wellness industry, real estate, coaching, and consulting.

From Tarot cards to strategy decks I blend design thinking and inspired action to create massive mindset breakthroughs and impact with my clients.

If you are ready to commit to becoming more of who you are with confidence, let's get started.

# Part I

# FOUNDATIONAL PRINCIPLES

*"The first, dazzling stage of faith is called bright faith. It is likened to sitting in a darkened room with the door closed, shut-in, and oppressed. Then for one reason or another, that door swings open. We may not see what is outside, but we know there is an outside. That means there is light, there is possibility, it's a far bigger world than what we might have gotten accustomed to."*

—**SHARON SALZBERG**, Buddhist teacher, and author

Chapter 1

# CREATIVITY

YOU'RE AT A MOMENT OF BRIGHT FAITH. YOU'RE TIRED of being tired. Bored of being bored. You see a tiny spark of possibility of who you are, a glimpse into your future. Your Clear Vision is that bright light, but it feels foreign, unfamiliar, and quite possibly scary. You don't know how to get from here to there, but you are ready.

Welcome to the Messy Middle—the space between who you are today and who you are becoming. Ready for the mind bender? Creativity is how you become more you.

Creativity isn't the final painting hanging in a museum; it's the day in and day out process of being creative. Creativity lives in the Messy Middle, in a land of uncertainty, and sometimes, quite frankly, confusion.

Creativity is the gateway between today and what is currently impossible—your Clear Vision.

## CREATIVITY

Draw a simple line graph with me. I know, math, but hang with me here.

Line graphs have two axes, the X- and Y-axis. The X-axis runs horizontally across the bottom; label it Time. The Y-axis vertically runs up and down the side; label it Energy. In the upper right corner at the very tippy-top add a dot, and label that "Clear Vision realized."

Most people live their lives by default, never exerting more energy than needed, so they move along the X-axis of Time. Sure, they are given promotions, maybe they get married, have children, and may genuinely be happy, though many people who live their lives by default aren't happy.

That thing is, at the end of the chart, when time runs out, you die. I hate to be so morbid, but it's the truth. You have one precious life, and your eyes will close for the final time sometime in the future. How you spend your time and energy between today and that moment in time is up to you.

Another way to live your life is to add Energy. The more you expand your energy, the more you can laser focus and move towards your Clear Vision. I'll share exactly how to expand your energy in Chapter 7.

Draw a straight line between today, at the 0-point of the chart, all the way up to the upper right corner, to connect today to your "Clear Vision realized." Logically, your brain thinks that you have to move through Time linearly and the

## FIND YOUR CLEAR VISION

fastest way to get there is in a straight line. Now label the space in between today and your Clear Vision realized as the Messy Middle.

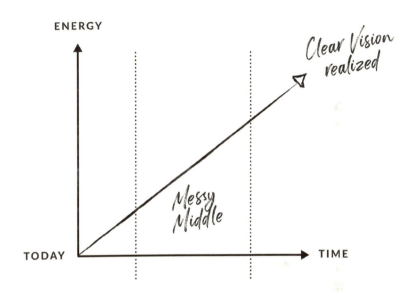

But life doesn't work in a linear fashion. Our energy ebbs and flows, and things get in the way. Draw a line that goes up and down like a snake weaving from high to low energy between today and your Clear Vision realized.

Each time your energy drops down, label it with all of the fears that come up when you think about creating your Clear Vision.

"This is dumb."

## CREATIVITY

"I'm going to look stupid."

"What if I fail?"

"It's going to be hard."

"I don't know how to do it."

On the top of the energy arch, label it with the juiciest feeling you can imagine when things go right, and you see yourself getting closer to your Clear Vision. I call these "pop thoughts" because you are popping your energy.

"I did it!"

"It's a miracle!"

"This is divine!"

"Cue the confetti!"

This is how our energy goes, up and down, not necessarily depending on the circumstance of the day, but depending on the feeling and emotional weight we give the moment.

Now draw a curved line that arches over the top of the Messy Middle, bypassing the ups and downs, that lands on your Clear Vision realized. This is the roadmap for your Clear Vision. Ideally, we want to stay elevated out of the Messy Middle by

## FIND YOUR CLEAR VISION

creating your Inner Platform, focused on your mindset, inner trust, self-awareness, and your Clear Vision.

Reinvention happens in the space between a failure and a miracle. It happens when you choose to stay the course and do the work to be creative, even in the Messy Middle. Are you ready?

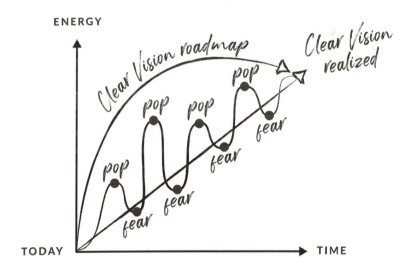

## WHAT IS CREATIVITY?

After I reinvented my career and started my coaching practice, an advertising executive asked, "Won't you miss being creative?"

## CREATIVITY

"No," I answered, and here's why. Creativity is not reserved for creative types. Creativity is not an exclusive club that only artists, painters, dancers, and poets have a membership to.

Creativity is choosing to be you, on purpose, every day.

Creativity is finding flow in the chaos of parenthood.

Creativity is heard in heated conversations and protest chants.

Creativity is seen in the arch of a flower stem in your kitchen window on a sunny morning.

Creativity is finding delight in the perfect blend of chia seed pudding and blackberries in your weekend brunch.

Creativity is felt in the energy you bring into a room.

Creativity is your quirks and eccentricities.

Creativity is an experience that can be seen, touched, and felt by others.

It's layered into your senses, weaving together a new experience day in and day out, to make you become more of who you are on purpose.

Creativity is the art of breaking down the barrier of who you think you are supposed to be and bringing to life more of who you are. Simply stated, it's reinventing you from the inside out.

It's a revolution that's taking place right now. You've caught a glimpse of who you are, through the door of bright faith, with the potential to be creative. And you are in luck because creativity is learned, practiced, and shared. You are welcome to join the revolution if you want, or stay on the default timeline. Again, your choice.

I've helped hundreds of businesses and people express who they choose to be through the creative process. I've witnessed my clients meet their creativity with tears in their eyes. Executive vice presidents in entertainment, senior vice presidents of brand strategy, lawyers, real estate agents, data scientists, creative directors, and spiritual leaders. Creativity is not an intangible talent reserved for artistic types; it's a state of mind that can be learned using a method called design thinking. As Maya Angelou reminds us, "You can't use up creativity. The more you use, the more you have."

## DESIGN THINKING

A creative mindset comes to life using a method called design thinking, and it is integral to building your creative power. Whether you're reinventing your mindset, career, or personal brand, using design thinking will give you agency to choose from curiosity rather than confusion, fun rather than fear.

Design thinking is the strategic process that design practitioners (like me when I was a graphic designer) use to make an idea real, to make the impossible come to life. Tom Kelley

## CREATIVITY

and David Kelley, two brothers who wrote the book, *Creative Confidence*, explain it this way: "Design thinking relies on the natural—and coachable—human ability to be intuitive, to recognize patterns and to construct ideas that are emotionally meaningful as well as functional."

Companies like Google and Apple use design thinking to create innovative solutions. DreamWorks and Universal use it to come up with fresh new ideas. Artists and designers use it to conceptualize art that hasn't been created yet. We're going to use design thinking to design your life. There are six steps.

1. Release Judgment

2. Brainstorm

3. Clear Vision

4. Laser Focus

5. Roadmap

6. Share

The creative process is like growing a garden. I'm not a gardener in any way, shape, or form. But I do know that to reap the rewards of a lush thriving garden, there are things you must do, in a certain order, to create the environment for Mother Nature to grow out of the ground.

## FIND YOUR CLEAR VISION

Before even thinking of putting the first seed in the ground, I need to release the inner critic in my head that tells me I'm not a good gardener. I may have grown up in the Midwest, but I am not a dirt-under-your-nails kind of gal. But that doesn't mean I can't learn how to do it.

To begin, I **release any judgment** I'm bringing into the thought of creating a garden.

- I don't have a green thumb.

- I can't grow anything, just look at my houseplants, wait, I don't have houseplants for a reason.

- My husband can garden—he should do it.

- What if nothing grows? This is going to be a colossal waste of time.

Notice these are just thoughts I'm bringing with me into the idea of the garden. I haven't even put seeds into the ground, and I'm already killing them.

After releasing any judgmental thoughts I have about what it means to be a gardener, I **brainstorm** ideas of what I want the garden to be.

- Is it a root vegetable garden?

- A flower garden?

## CREATIVITY

- One that attracts butterflies and hummingbirds?

- One that blooms year-round?

- The possibilities are endless!

Next, I paint a picture in my head, or on paper, of my **clear future vision**—what I want the garden to look like. I can't see the garden; it's only dirt at this point, but I know I can place seeds in a certain order and potentially they'll pop up in that order, or maybe not, but I can see the vision in my head. I know what I want, and I know where I am headed.

Now that I have a Clear Vision of the possibility, I **laser focus** on making it happen. I plant the seeds, water them, and keep the rabbits and deer away from them. And it grows with my nurturing, caring, and tending to.

Add water, sunshine, remove the weeds, and stay committed to the future vision. That's the **roadmap**.

Will it turn out just the way I planned it? Probably not; it's a gift from Mother Nature. I'm not going to question her plan, but I do know what will happen if I *don't* tend to it...nothing. It will stay the same patch of dirt that it started as when I began.

Let's break down each step of design thinking so you learn how to embody this new way of thinking in your reinvention to design your life from the inside out.

# FIND YOUR CLEAR VISION

## Step 1: Release Judgment

It's easier to paint a picture with a blank canvas. The problem is, you're in a mess of your own making, oftentimes being your own worst enemy when it comes to your reinvention. You'll stop yourself, get scared, try too hard, or fail and start over, carrying the baggage of past failure into the next attempt.

Your canvas is textured and gray, substantially layered with all the reasons why you "can't do it." Instead, focus on "Why not? Let's do it!" Releasing your judgment of how life is supposed to go may be your biggest hurdle in reinvention.

But does reinvention need to be hard? What if it was easy? What if it was possible to release the stories of "why not" and start with a clean canvas infused with life-supporting energy? In Chapter 5 I'll show you how to identify the limiting beliefs, which form your Paradox Pattern, and then in Chapter 7 we'll look at the habits and rituals to release the gray fuzzy buzz of your Paradox Pattern to move forward with a clear canvas.

## Step 2: Brainstorm

Brainstorming generates wild audacious ideas, intentions, and goals. Be open for crazy spiritual connections and consequences, déjà vu moments, kismet moments, and instant creative downloads. We don't need to know how we're going to create the wild ideas that pop up out of the blue—but it's the most exciting thing you've thought of in years, right? In

# CREATIVITY

the brainstorming phase, we allow for the storm—the crazy whirlwind of ideas—to spill over the edges.

I'll teach you how to take the 50,000-foot view, so you can witness what's not working in your life, and what needs to change so you can be your reinvention every day.

To embody this step of the creative mindset, I imagine you standing with both feet grounded into the earth, firmly planted like roots connecting you to safety and security so you can elevate your mind by throwing your hands up to the sky, open and receptive to all possibilities.

We're going to learn how to awaken your energy through chakras, breathwork, and even rewiring neural pathways to try on new ideas, because if you can't dream big enough you are going to bore yourself to death, both now and in the future.

## Step 3: Clear Vision

As I mentioned, I grew up in the Midwest where tornadoes were a weekly occurrence in late summer. Tornadoes are small-scale storms that produce the fastest winds on earth. A single-vortex tornado, like the one you see in the movie *The Wizard of Oz*, is theorized to have a calm center called the "eye of the storm."

In a world of chaos and confusion, your Clear Vision is the eye of the storm. Creativity, imagination, magic, and fun live there. It's your north star, the bright dazzling light that you can hang on to when everything else seems to be swirling out of control.

Your Clear Vision can be as big as a new career, starting a business, or leaving a relationship. It can be as small as a poem or a sticky note. It's a future that you can see and hold space for in the present moment even though it's not currently "real."

Visioning is a powerful tool for creatives because it's coming up with an idea that doesn't yet exist. It's what creatives do: make ideas real.

In Chapter 3 I'll teach you how to stay in the eye of the storm longer by using your Inner Platform of inner trust, self-awareness, and mindset and anchoring into your Clear Vision so you can practice dreaming big and believing in yourself. And there is an entire chapter, Chapter 6, dedicated to taking you through the Clear Vision framework so you can find your vision and make it real.

Until you practice being in the eye of the storm it's scary because your logical side wants to say, "This is impossible! I'll die of embarrassment, failure, or stupidity. It's a tornado for God's sake, find a storm shelter—*QUICK!*" If those thoughts pop up in your mind when you start to practice visioning, go back to Step 1 and release your judgment. It's all part of the process.

## Step 4: Laser Focus

You have a to-do list a mile long. Is there one thing on there that is for your personal growth? One thing, that if you started today, it would multiply over time to create your future vision? More than likely the answer is no, and here's why: most people are not willing to commit to creating change, much less transformation.

The single ingredient to create focus is to commit. Brainstorming had us in the clouds: creating, visioning, and dreaming. Now we are coming back down to earth to focus and create.

Commit to one idea, one vision, one mission, one concept for a determined time frame. One week, one year, it doesn't matter. Focus is when you choose to move forward towards your vision, not away from it. You choose to make choices that are aligned with creating that vision, not sabotaging it.

After I brainstorm, I take one idea and save all of the other wild and crazy ideas on a Google doc called "Ideas for Later." I want you to create one as well. This is the space to house all the other thoughts—like "but maybe I should…," or "that may be a good idea…"—that try to sneak in and throw you off course of your vision.

More ideas aren't bad, but the brain has a hard time focusing on too many ideas at once; that's why we aren't wired to multi-task. Multi-tasking is doing two things at 50 percent. Imagine if you tried to create all of your ideas at once. You'd be giving each idea 10 percent time, energy, and effort. It won't work.

Focus is fueled by rituals, habits, and an energy plan which is foundational to expanding your energy to help you laser focus. Once you have built a ritualized practice and you can expand your energy and laser focus, then we map it out.

## Step 5: Roadmap

You have the vision and the focus, and now you need the plan—how to make the idea real. Your roadmap is the path between today and your Clear Vision realized, alive, and kicking in real life.

Have you ever been asked the dreaded interview question, "Where do you want to be in two to five years?"

Who can answer that? People who have committed to their future vision.

Who can't? People who are surviving, not thriving, with multiple responsibilities—to themselves, their family, or their career, but who have no Clear Vision.

Five years is a long time, but tomorrow is not. Tomorrow always comes. There are twelve months in a year, about thirty days in a month, four weeks a month, seven days a week, and twenty-four hours a day. What's your plan?

## CREATIVITY

Don't have one?

Cool. Most people don't—which is why people say, "Time flies" or "Where did the time go?"

Without a roadmap, people are more likely to stay on the default timeline of their life. With a roadmap, we know where we are going and how to get there.

Staying on track is going to challenge you. You want to see results now, get it done, and move on. I've seen that movie, and I know how that turns out for you. You don't buckle your seat belt once and expect it will keep you safe the next time you get in the car, and you don't brush your teeth once and expect not to get cavities.

It's pretty simple when you think about it. Create a plan and stick to it.

There are many different methods to hack your productivity, or stick to a workout schedule, or even stay on track to write a book, for example. Through a lot of trial and error, I've found that the best way to create my vision is to break it into massive, macro, micro, and mini-steps, which you will learn how to do in Chapter 6.

Like it or not we are multi-passionate people with multiple responsibilities. In order to create big things, sometimes we need a big calendar. I use a large paper calendar for my kids' activities, with colored reminders in Google Calendar.

## FIND YOUR CLEAR VISION

I also have a monthly and daily paper calendar with large projects and room to brainstorm, as well as a to-do list in Apple Notes. It's a blend that works for me, and the smaller steps allow me to manage my expectations and not feel as if I need to do it all. Instead, I've created a method that helps me stay focused on massive, macro, micro, and mini-steps towards my vision.

A roadmap, whether it's on paper, a Google Doc, a checklist digitally (or otherwise) is a landing place to keep you focused on the day-to-day and hold space for your bird's-eye view.

## Step 6: Share

Sharing your personal and professional reinvention shows up in a lot of different ways.

People will start to notice a shift in who you are being. Maybe it's your calm presence during a stressful moment. Or how you carry yourself in meetings you are being asked to lead. Maybe it's the aliveness you embody because you're spending your weekends in the studio painting. Hell, maybe it's your glowing skin because you made hydration a daily priority.

You will start to share your vision naturally. It will come up in conversations because people will want to know what's changed about you. You'll start speaking from a place of inner trust and confidence, which will attract new opportunities and connections.

## CREATIVITY

I'll teach you how to create your Visionary Values so you'll know exactly what to share because sharing is what makes someone with a Clear Vision become a visionary.

You can be the most creative, amazing person and never share. Cool. I totally get it. But my guess is that you're reading this book because that's not you, and you are called to create something bigger than yourself. You are here to be a vessel for expansion and possibility because you want to make an impact and leave a legacy in this world. You just need a guide. This book is your guide. Welcome to the adventure of your lifetime.

What it means to be a professional is radically changing. You are at a crossroads, a bright moment of faith to release the past and create the future. And to do that you simply need to stay in the Messy Middle longer.

The world is getting smaller and larger at the same time; it's the paradox in which we live. It's a mess of media messages, unrealistic expectations, and outdated corporate structures. In a world where you are told you need to be "successful," creating a Clear Vision and anchoring into your Inner Platform is how you can create your life by design. It's the answer to lifting you higher than what you thought possible in your career, livelihood, and your fulfillment as a creative person.

We are killing the limiting belief of "creativity is only for creatives," killing the starving artist stereotype, killing the hair-brained scientist who can't find their glasses, killing the glorification of busy. We are getting comfortable with being uncomfortable longer, living in the unknown, and trusting ourselves in the process.

I encourage you to journal—no, scribble—your ideas and insights in the margins of the book. It's your living journal, the beginning of your roadmap to reinvention.

Chapter 2

# FEMININE AND MASCULINE ENERGY

I WAS GIVEN THE OPPORTUNITY TO PITCH AN IDEA FOR a TEDx Talk. The concept of the talk was going to be "What's next?" Ideas were like popcorn in my head. I was copying and pasting the TEDx application into a Google Doc and filling in the vital information before I thought, "Wait, pause, Lisa. Close the laptop right now. Is this aligned with my vision for the next three months?"

The talk was going to be a few days after the New Year, which meant I would be rehearsing throughout the holiday season. Did I really want to do that?

That summer, I had started my podcast and was writing this book. I wanted to have a magical holiday with my kids. They were getting older, and the twinkle in their eye on Christmas morning was not going to be there forever.

## FEMININE AND MASCULINE ENERGY

My masculine energy jumped into action, wanting the challenge and recognition of being a TEDx speaker.

My feminine energy desired space, flow, and family.

I put down my laptop, stepped away, and went to sleep. The next day I called a friend. I made the choice not to submit an application and instead save it on my "Ideas for Later" list. It took a full twenty-four hours for me to choose to align to my vision for the next three months instead of doing what was the default for me—choosing professional work over personal time.

The three steps I took were deliberate: close my computer, sleep, and call a friend. All are practices I rely on to help me choose outside of my default pattern, which is woven with ambition, drive, and professional recognition. My mind plays tricks on me, and without the self-awareness to simply close my computer and step away, I would be leading a very different life, one without balance and deep relationships with friends, family, and, most importantly, my kids.

Creating a life by design happens in small choices. It's when who you are and what you do is interwoven into your mind, body, soul, and the choices you make. It's a braided union between creative energy—your feminine energy and masculine energy—which is the container for a holistic whole-self strategy.

**FIND YOUR CLEAR VISION**

## LIFE BY DESIGN USING THE HOLISTIC WHOLE-SELF STRATEGY

A holistic whole-self strategy is when there is no separation between who you are and what you do. Your mind, body, and soul are in union with how you make choices. You are led with integrity and intention, meaning your thoughts, speaking, and actions are in alignment with their highest and best decision-making.

Feminine energy—filled with habits, rituals, and connection to your most vibrant self—leads your creative side, and masculine energy—filled with systems and structure and get-it-done energy—provides the roadmap.

The holistic whole-self leaves you living in harmony with feminine and masculine energy which gives your Inner Platform structure to grow. Whether you identify as female, male, non-binary, or somewhere in between, you have feminine and masculine energetic traits. Let's explore why harmony is important.

Companies want leaders who can solve creative problems, which is the definition of feminine thinking plus masculine execution. Dream up the blue-sky idea and make it happen. Here are a few examples of leaders who approach their life (and leadership for that matter) using a holistic whole-self strategy.

## FEMININE AND MASCULINE ENERGY

Gwyneth Paltrow's million-dollar lifestyle company, Goop, bloomed from her curiosity of spiritual practices. She holds space for feminine exploration in a masculine business structure.

Mindy Kaling brought her flavor of feminine comedy to *The Office* when she was twenty-four years old. She knew how she wanted to express her creativity, in her own voice, and worked hard to make it happen.

Jonathan VanNess, a non-binary celebrity, famous for his bubbly creative energy on the show *Queer Eye*, expresses his creativity through fashion, hairstyling, grooming, and his social and politically curious podcast and Netflix show, *Getting Curious with Jonathan VanNess*. In 2019 he met Nancy Pelosi at the White House, in heels and a skirt. Love that!

Here are some other examples of people who live a holistic whole-self life.

One of my clients is the co-founder of a financial advisory firm, which is a traditionally male-dominated field. She connects to her spirit through daily yoga and affirmations.

Another client is the only female partner at a marketing agency specializing in real estate development. She is also a master life coach.

Another is a professional artist who loves creating spreadsheets to organize her materials.

### FIND YOUR CLEAR VISION

And finally, another client is a tenacious lawyer in a D.C. law firm who connects to her feminine energy through meditation, breathwork, and Tarot card readings.

Traditional leadership models are broken. Traditional pathways to success are bogus. The corporate ladder doesn't lead to happiness. We no longer have to create a life that separates who we are and what we do. It's in the union of both sides of ourselves that happiness is found.

Now is the time to create what it means to be fully you, claim your feminine creative energy, express it unapologetically, and live your life by design.

The problem is we've been led by energy based on self-preservation, getting it done, and protecting me and mine. It's pushing energy to survive. And hey, it's got us to where we are today, but it won't get us to where we want to go. The imbalance of masculine and feminine energy will only strengthen the polarity of the traditional belief structures we've grown up in, and we see where that road leads: to burnout and unhappiness.

And pushing survival energy isn't working anymore. It doesn't feel good, and it only gets you more of the same. You don't want to be defined by the past. You crave to be in harmony in your mind, body, and soul.

You may be thinking, "But Lisa, feminine energy? I'm a little worried I'm going to end up a hippie—barefoot, dressed in a white flowy linen dress, chanting in a drum circle with strangers. I'm a professional, and I like being a professional. How do I blend my feminine and masculine energy in a way that works for me?"

Don't worry, I've got you.

## WHAT IS MASCULINE ENERGY?

Masculine energy thrives in logical, rational decision-making. It wants to produce, not from a creative place, but instead, from the "let's get 'er done and move on" mentality.

Masculine energy has us high on caffeine, with the jitters, making snap decisions based on logic and righteousness, from the mindset that "only my logic is logical." It has *us* being right and *them* being wrong. We're armed with complexity and competition, having to do it all ourselves to feel steady, secure, and safe. There is nothing more satisfying to masculine energy than being in control. It's lonely energy masked in a complex structure with tunnel vision on being safe.

Cultural norms of what it means to be masculine have women working to be little men, smaller versions of masculinity, striving to work harder, better, and faster. It has women believing they have to do it all on their own because asking for help is a sign of weakness, proving that they just don't have what it takes to "make it in this world."

Masculine energy creates a paradoxical thought pattern that productivity results in success which will make you happy. The paradox is that there's always more work to be done so there's no time to be happy.

Don't get me wrong—there are also benefits to your masculine energy. It provides structure, planning, and the steadiness needed to live in our corporate world. Its tunnel vision enables you to laser focus.

Just because the collective consciousness has us believing that faster is better and working hard leads to success doesn't mean it's true. It's a thought that we hold as true. Masculine leadership has consumed us for too long, and no longer works.

## WHAT IS FEMININE ENERGY?

Feminine energy flourishes the intangible, non-linear feeling of joy, beauty, and flow. It wants to explore, play, and discover. Feminine energy dabbles without a deadline, putters around the house, questioning old ideas and playing with new ones. She's curious about ideas that don't make sense, willing to stay in the unknown because it's filled with possibilities and novelty. She is explorative, open, playful, and—dare I say—fun.

She's mothering—nourishing herself and others. She reaches out, holds hands, and cries with loved ones. And, oh my goodness, she loves.

## FEMININE AND MASCULINE ENERGY

Feminine energy holds space, patiently waiting for you to stay in the unknown of "What ifs?" and "Why not?" and "Oh, that looks like fun, let's try it out." She is open to inspiration without judgment and failing without shame.

Feminine energy is led by intuition, a knowing that transcends logic and science, and a connection to your highest self. Intuition is a wise woman who loves unconditionally. She's expansive, open, and connected to the world from a place of love and compassion. It's never-ending because it's sourced by your energy.

Feminine energy is what creativity is made of. She embodies the creative process of releasing judgment, brainstorming with her heart and soul, and declaring a Clear Vision from an elevated place of possibility without knowing how to do it.

When you are busy thinking, planning, producing, and trying to do it all on your own, your feminine energy is floating just above your busy little brain, filled with love and joy wondering when you are going to look up from your desk and notice her.

Recently a client texted me these words: "I've been doing some end of the year reflection and New Year planning and felt like the planning was masculine, despite meditating. Any guidance for how to plan for the year in a more feminine way?"

I replied, "Go outside and dream. And before you go to sleep, or right when you wake up, pay attention to how you feel. Plan for feelings instead of goals."

## FIND YOUR CLEAR VISION

EQ and IQ skills have become popular with different corporate assessments, trying to define your feminine energy and stick her into a line-by-line structure. Corporate leadership has defined feminine energy as "soft" skills. Feminine energy doesn't follow a hard and fast structure.

I had a discovery session with a new client whose employer told her she needed more executive presence and soft skills. I asked, "What would I see if you brought your feminine energy to your work?"

And she said, "Lisa, I don't have time to talk about feminine energy. I need soft skills like how to be flexible and connect with others."

Feminine energy *is* connection, flexibility, and embodies softness. Again, this is where corporate America has leadership all wrong. This is why we are here to reinvent.

Creative people—hell, everyone can benefit from the holistic whole-self strategy to unify their masculine and feminine energy and become their fullest, most vibrant self. This is how creatives bring new ideas from "out of nowhere" and make them real. The Inner Platform is a container to hold space for both sides of you, all of you. Built on the pillars of inner trust, self-awareness, and expanded energy, it's a safe playground to be both/and, not either/or.

## FEMININE AND MASCULINE ENERGY

# YOU CAN BE BOTH MASCULINE AND FEMININE

You can be:

vulnerable and strong

empathetic and enraged

humble and hot

soft and steady

stable and spontaneous

magical and logical

seeking and grounded

powerful and personable

How can you create space for both sides of you? For all of you? Because you, my friend, are you everywhere you go.

The creative process is the ultimate blend of masculine and feminine energy; it's dreaming of the unknown, playing in its messy, unconstructed round and curvy form, and giving it structure.

True co-creation with masculine and feminine energy is when you are open to receiving creativity and willing to follow the absurd idea while moving steadily through a process. It's the power of expanded energy with laser focus.

Artist and musician Jill Scott released *Who Is Jill Scott?* when she was twenty-seven years old. In a podcast with Jemele Hill, she said, "How do I explain this? I just did something that came from my heart, it wasn't a bunch of rocket science or a bunch of producers around telling me what I should do or how I should do, I was just doing it because that's the way I felt. Even now I listen to it, and I think, 'It's pretty damn good.'"

Creativity is not something reserved for musicians, content creators, or founders in black turtlenecks. Creativity is available and waiting for you to take the first step into the tornado. The adventure is calling. The vision is inside of you, in your eye of the storm. The first step in your reinvention is to be willing to take the first step.

# Part II

# YOUR INNER PLATFORM

*"Pain pushes until vision pulls."*

–DR. MICHAEL BECKWITH

Chapter 3

# MOVE FROM BREAKDOWN TO BREAKTHROUGH

IN 2012 I WAS SUED FOR COPYRIGHT INFRINGEMENT. Bottom line, I was sued for presenting my false identity, the story of who I thought I was supposed to be to the world.

My branding studio, Step Brightly, helped businesses create and execute their brands with intention. I primarily worked with women-owned businesses, or, as I like to call them, "businesses in the business of women"—like fashion lines, makers, and wellness studios.

On my website's blog, I would curate delightfully eclectic spaces, bright colors, detailed patterns, and event imagery I found on Pinterest. The blog was great for SEO (search engine optimization) and was an easy way for clients to see Step

Brightly's style. My studio was featured on Apartment Therapy, West Elm, and many other event and lifestyle blogs.

I would cite my sources and give praise, naively thinking that showing them love through back-linking and a "Look at this gorgeous photo by..." was enough because, at the time, it was common practice to have mood boards on your website. If everybody was doing it, why couldn't I?

I remember opening the crisp #10 envelope and reading the formal letter filled with legal jargon as my stomach flipped and soured. I was being sued for copyright infringement because of a single image on my website without my having paid for the license to use it, and they were back-charging me for the time it was live, which amounted to about $3,000 USD.

I reached out to my friend and founder of Creative Genius Law, Patrice Perkins. She told me there was no way around it. I had to pay in full and take down not just that image but all images on my site that I didn't own or had permission to use.

"That's literally 85 percent of my blog. I'm in the visual design business for God's sake!"

I was crushed, embarrassed, and mortified. I spent weeks furious at myself, ruminating with my Paradox Pattern and feeling like a fraud, which brought up every imposter syndrome moment of "Who are you? You're not a branding expert, you can't even take care of your own damn business!"

## FIND YOUR CLEAR VISION

I was an amateur, a phony, and a thief who had to pay $3,000 and all of my self-esteem. Trying to fit in and look like a trendy design studio had created a false mask of creativity, prestige, and confidence. I had been stealing other people's images and putting them on my website to "represent" me and my artfully crafted lifestyle.

As I sat with the realization of what was happening to my sense of self, I looked under the surface and realized I was terrified of being judged. The formal crisp white letter was the trigger that led to thoughts of how I was showing up in my business, which wasn't me. That #10 envelope cracked open the mask I was using to hide behind because I didn't see the power in just being me as a creative entrepreneur.

I created a façade of fitting in just enough to be noticed for my work, but not stand out too much, because God forbid I rub someone the wrong way and get called out for it. This way of being "just enough" was showing up everywhere in my life: I would charge just enough so people would work with me. I would dress just enough so people would notice me, but not too much.

What a convenient place to wallow in a bunch of bullshit.

At the moment of my breakdown, I paused. I breathed. I listened. That small voice inside my heart said, "Hey Lisa, wouldn't it be more fun to hire a photographer and shoot your own stuff?" It wasn't groundbreaking, but it sounded like a possibility.

Pausing into the quiet moment in between my thoughts and feelings broke the pattern of my Paradox. We'll dive more into identifying your Paradox in the next chapter. For now, just know that your Paradox Pattern is a series of repeated neural pathways formed by stories you hold as true that have been on repeat for decades, creating thoughts and feelings that are hardwired into your brain.

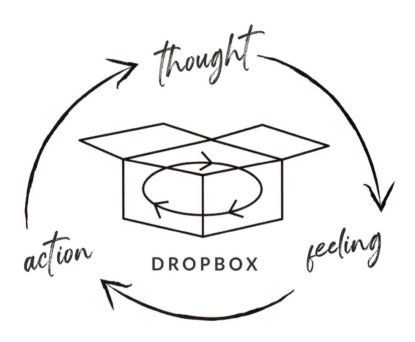

Your Paradox has you boxed in the universal loop of drama, a dropbox with four sides built on your cultural upbringing, your self-identity, what you believe to be true, and self-doubt. When you are stuck in your dropbox, it's a loop of drama and

## FIND YOUR CLEAR VISION

fear, leaving no room for creating a future vision outside of what your Paradox currently holds as true.

For example, your cultural upbringing has taught you to believe something is true: "Don't wear your heart on your sleeve."

You've identified that thought as truth. "I shouldn't share my feelings because I'll get hurt."

But then something happens and you start to doubt its validity. "Wait, when I shared from my heart, it felt good."

And then something inside of you changes. What you have thought in the past, what's worked so far, isn't going to work anymore. The small window of self-doubt in the dropbox is your opportunity to choose another thought. "Maybe it's okay to share from my heart."

When you break the thought, you break the pattern and break through.

In moments of chaos, we choose another thought. When the world is broken, turned upside down, and fear is running high, the foundation of your Paradox is shaky, energy is disrupted, and you feel uncertain. You may feel pissed, sad, heartbroken, or feel like an idiot. But something needs to break. Typically it's your thinking, so energy can move. It's time to elevate out of the dropbox and liberate your thinking, no longer taking for granted "that's just the way it is" thinking.

## MOVE FROM BREAKDOWN TO BREAKTHROUGH

In the movies this is the moment the clouds part, birds sing, and you run off into the sunset because you have been found! *Redeemed! Reborn! Transformed!* But it doesn't always happen like that. Sometimes we stay in the dropbox for a long long time. We bounce back and forth, and side-to-side around the dropbox because it's within our comfort zone. I could have edited out all of the images I didn't own on my blog. Sure, that would have been fine, and that may have been easier than shooting all of my own content, but that would have been within the universal dropbox of my Paradox Pattern—needing to show up perfectly to prove I'm valuable.

Instead, I chose to listen to the small voice, and claim agency of who I wanted to be outside of the dropbox of fitting in. Transformation is a choice, one that requires practice and care.

What if you didn't believe the thoughts that you are not enough anymore?

When you have had enough of playing inside the dropbox, you pop. To pop means you have left the dropbox and all of the drama you had previously identified as true and are now thinking outside the box. Creative thoughts, novelty, and your Clear Vision are found in the pop. Sometimes it's that easy—simply to choose another thought and move directly from the drop to the pop. And sometimes we move from the drop into the Messy Middle and, once again, get stuck. And, my friend, this is where we start our journey into the Inner Platform.

## FIND YOUR CLEAR VISION

Your Messy Middle is the gateway between what is currently impossible in your dropbox and living your life by design in the pop. So, what is the Inner Platform, you ask? Is it like the diving board of the soul? Not really.

In marketing terms, a "platform" is the framework to connect your business to our audience through social media, advertising, and other messaging. Your Inner Platform, built on a creative mindset plus self-awareness, inner trust, and elevated energy, is the framework to connect you to your Clear Vision. I suppose you could say your Inner Platform is like a springboard into your future, because when you start to play with and practice your self-awareness and inner trust and start elevating your energy, you are able to dive into your Clear Vision with confidence and conviction. You may not land the perfect backflip every time, but you are willing to practice, take the leap, and get wet.

Bouncing around the dropbox of my "I need to prove I'm perfect so I'm valuable" thinking was exhausting. So, I invented a new game: My Clear Vision.

I reinvented how I was approaching business, and even more importantly, who I wanted to be as an entrepreneur, the CEO of my business, and in my overall life: I became a badass, magic-making, lightbulb of ideas.

There is nothing more unique, raw, real, intelligent, or authentic than you when you are connected to your Clear Vision, which expresses itself as trust. Inner trust is a way of being, and you can't trust yourself if you are pieced together by thin strands of your Paradox's silk web.

Reframing the thought that I was an imposter to fully embracing what I had to offer would attract the right people and opportunities to me, because I was sharing who I was without the paradoxical mask of "how the industry does it" or trying to look perfect. This is the epicenter of creativity, the moment of reinvention.

Are you showing up as you? Or hiding behind someone else's version of who you think you should be? What is it truly costing you to show up that way? $3,000? $30,000? More?

## HOW TO POP: THE WHITE SPACE BETWEEN THOUGHTS AND BELIEFS

Have you ever read a book about spirituality or finding your purpose, and they tell you to "let it go"?

"Let those thoughts go."

"Let that frustration go."

"Let it go," said Elsa.

I can't tell you how frustrated this makes me. What am I supposed to let go? What am I letting it go for? Where is it going? How do I actually do that? I have so many questions.

## FIND YOUR CLEAR VISION

Here's the catch. It's not actually that you are releasing something that you can tangibly hold and throw into the trash. If we spent all of our time trying to identify what we wanted to throw away, we'd be really busy making lists, checking with others, and putting outdated ideas that no longer fit into garbage bags in the attic "just in case."

Instead, let's think of "letting go" as "trying on" a new thought. And in order to try something on, we need to have an open mind for what may happen when we try it on, so we'll create white space for something new, like a new thought.

Creating white space is something that designers, artists, and writers do to spark new ideas. White space is a design element where the designer purposefully adds a blank space on the page or the website for your eyes to rest on, or to make you pause on a specific area of the design.

It's a pregnant pause.

A moment to rest.

A space in between.

White space is the space in your mind between your thoughts and your feelings.

You can change your brain using neuroplasticity, which means you can signal new thoughts to create new choices. Change the way you think and feel, and you change your life.

## MOVE FROM BREAKDOWN TO BREAKTHROUGH

White space has you asking, "What if..." and getting curious to look a little deeper. For example, "What if I didn't dread going to work on Monday?"

Insert white space.

Insert a pause.

A breath.

Try on a new thought: "That's interesting! Maybe we should explore that. What if I didn't dread Mondays? What would that be like?"

White space is the space in between thoughts and ideas. When we are told to "let it go" we need to create a little more wiggle room between our pattern and the next thought we choose.

That little bit of wiggle room—the space in between thoughts, feelings, and action—is self-awareness. Boom, that's it. You are self-aware.

You've opened up a little more space inside of that massive brain of yours to choose outside of your pattern, to pop outside of the drop. The heart of self-awareness is noticing your thoughts. Then you get to choose: do I go with the thought on the right or the left?

Having the courage to choose a new thought is radical. This is the first step to finding your Clear Vision.

**FIND YOUR CLEAR VISION**

Imagine that you are tasked with a new client at work. It's an exciting client, someone on the cutting edge of innovation, something you're interested in pursuing, and you know this is going to be great for your reputation at the company.

So you start to brainstorm. You talk with your colleagues, pick up some reading materials for inspiration, but then you notice that a lot of the ideas you are coming up with are the same. They aren't that exciting, and you start to feel like you are going in circles. You think that you might not have a new idea; self-doubt looms, and your dropbox starts to get tighter.

Your co-workers are throwing out ideas left and right, and you start comparing yourself to them. So you try to power through and keep pushing, thinking that if you pushed harder, you might crack open a new idea. You also recognized this hasn't worked in the past, and "powering through" leaves you exhausted. So why is it going to work now? Defeated, you throw your hands up in frustration at 11 pm the night before the client meeting and head home, only to toss and turn all night.

You're in the dropbox—bouncing around in self-doubt, worry, and trying to solve a new problem from old energy.

While you're busy burning the midnight oil inside of your dropbox, you don't notice the top of the box is open. You've been so busy trying to work with what you've got, trying to work within the limitations of who you currently are and the thoughts you currently have, that you haven't thought to look up.

*Ahem.* Why do you think they call self-awareness witnessing yourself from 50,000 feet?

You decide to take a peek out of the box. You let out a big sigh, take a deep breath, center your thoughts, and close your eyes to alert your subconscious that it's okay to rest for a moment. And you feel yourself rising out of the box. And as your mind, body, and soul rise out of the box, you're able to see and feel a bright light shining on you. You absorb that light, that energy, that clarity. It connects to a deeper power source within you as if you've literally been turned on. And when you open your eyes, you realize there is a world of possibilities in this new energy field. The energy you have created is now flowing from you as the source of a new form of creativity—yours.

White space is the tool to pop out of your dropbox. Clients pay me to guide them to this singular moment when they move from the drop to the pop. It's a gift to behold.

## CHOOSE AGAIN

Here are a handful of questions that will help you pop out of the dropbox by adding a little more white space into your thinking.

When you are in a breakdown, your Paradox thrives. It literally lights up because it believes it is protecting you. Once your Paradox is triggered, come hell or high water, it's going to prove its purpose: to protect your dropbox thinking; that's the game it's playing.

**FIND YOUR CLEAR VISION**

Here's the opportunity. You can continue to play that game. Absolutely, have fun. I did it for years. Or, instead (this is going to sound simplistic to those of you that love to have trend reports and data charts to make decisions from)…you pause.

I want you to pause, close your eyes, and breathe. Notice your breath. It's only going to take maybe one or two breaths—that's it. I'm not asking you to meditate for ten minutes. I'm asking you to take two breaths.

One.

Two.

This is your opportunity to choose outside of what you think may be true. Instead, ask yourself,

"What would it be like to believe in me? 100 percent believe in me?"

"Who gets to decide how I want to be in the world?"

That's right. You do.

And we're still breathing.

"From this point forward, who do I want to be?"

Consider placing a hand on your heart or your pointer finger about one inch above the space between your eyes; this is your third eye chakra. Rest your hand or finger there and ask:

## MOVE FROM BREAKDOWN TO BREAKTHROUGH

"Do I want to feel this way? Do I want to be at the mercy of these thoughts?"

No, probably not.

"How do I want to feel?"

What words pop to mind for you?

Loving

Caring

Calm

Thoughtful

Playful

Brave

Sexy

Fun

Clear

Emboldened?

Tell me three reasons why you should be this way.

## FIND YOUR CLEAR VISION

We don't need to know how to do it. We just want to know that you have the desire. We are going to get curious by asking our most vibrant self, our third eye, what it desires.

Asking questions and listening is the first step in having a breakthrough. We simply have to listen a little bit longer.

White space opens up the space for newness, and what's not predictable for you. Because, listen, if your future vision is predictable, then it's still in your dropbox. Your Clear Vision lives outside of what is predictable for you and is no longer living by cause and effect.

You are your biggest asset. Showing up online, in your business, career, or in any outer expression, as anyone else, or with any hesitation, is a Paradox Pattern that will bite you in your ass. Hanging on to thoughts of self-doubt will only create more self-doubt.

Give yourself white space to think outside the box and stretch into the Messy Middle with inner trust and self-awareness that you can handle the unknown. Be willing to try on new ideas, and rely on trusting yourself through the Messy Middle. This is where visionaries are born.

Many people will say, "I'll believe it when I see it"—which means they will be stuck in their dropbox waiting for someone else to lead. You are that leader—you are the belief of a future vision that is bigger and brighter than you have ever dared to imagine. Now hold on to that new thought because we are going to release everything that no longer serves you.

Breathe.

One.

Two.

Chapter 4

# IDENTIFYING YOUR PARADOX PATTERN

A PARADOX IS A STATEMENT THAT, DESPITE SOUNDING reasonable, leads to a conclusion that seems senseless or self-contradictory.

A pattern is a repetitive graphic technique used in design to increase visual excitement by creating surface-level interest and enhancing the user experience.

Your Paradox Pattern is a series of repeated neural pathways formed by stories you hold as true. These stories have been on repeat for decades, creating thoughts, feelings, and actions that are hardwired into your brain. As a result, your Paradox Pattern is preventing you from changing, growing, and, at the end of the day, limiting what's possible for you.

## IDENTIFYING YOUR PARADOX PATTERN

It's a looping record of the past on repeat. And, spoiler alert: the original story that started this whole-she-bang? It isn't true.

My client, Brianna, excels at strategically creative work as the EVP of advertising at her agency. She's the go-to person when it comes to fixing a teetering client relationship. When the client's not happy, then bring in Brianna. Her superpower has quickly moved her up the agency ranks, but for her, there's no real joy in soothing a relationship. It's all a dog-and-pony show. But she's good at it and gets paid a lot to do it.

She works tons of hours, has one darling little girl, and a working husband. She's a perfectionist in work and play, overachieving in everything, including her workouts, children's activities, and her daily glass of wine or two.

She finds herself spending all of her brain power at work, which leaves her exhausted when she comes home to her family. Brianna's "always on" energy leaves her overextended and needing major emotional and physical recovery on the weekends when she'd rather be playing with her daughter. Going at 200 percent all the time, and quickly crashing to 0, leaves her daughter guessing, "Which Mommy am I going to get today?"

She expects perfection of herself because she's afraid of losing a client, which, in her mind, would mean she's no longer valuable. Yet, with all of the external success, she is left unsure of her future. She's started to recognize that what got her to where she is today is only going to get more of the same: overextended, exhausted, and emotionally unavailable.

"Is this all there is in life?" she wonders.

She feels like she has no wiggle room to grow or even consider taking on more responsibilities. Her husband wants to have another child, and she can't fathom what that would look like. It's exhausting for her to even think about it.

Brianna's biggest fear is that she is only valuable because of the "corporate work" she does, and if she doesn't give it her all, emotionally, physically and at 200 percent, she won't be needed.

Brianna identifies as a powerhouse executive, the Olivia Pope of the Client Relationship World. But her identity is starting to crack, and she's scared. She fears that if she slows down, or explores what else is possible, she'll lose control, mess up, or fail. "If I'm not perfect, who am I?" she asks herself.

Have you ever felt that if you slowed down, messed up, failed, or took time off, you wouldn't be valuable?

I asked Brianna, "How much longer are you willing to run your life this way?"

Your Paradox Pattern is a seemingly never-ending Ferris wheel.

## IDENTIFYING YOUR PARADOX PATTERN

The power needed to turn the Ferris wheel round and round is found in the constant need to prove yourself as a valid human being through masculine leadership traits: ambition, validation, competition, drive, and logic.

It's fueled by self-doubt, because you, as someone who values love, compassion, and connection, recognize the absurdity of it all.

Inside your Paradox Pattern you feel the Ferris wheel's rusty hospital green cabin rocking side to side. You're stuck in this infinite loop, trying not to throw up, thinking the cabin door is locked. But, if you look closer, it's not. The latch is hanging open. You are locked in a paradox of your own making, and it's time to stand up and step out.

## THE PROBLEM OF A PARADOX

Your Paradox lurks around many areas of your life, not just at work. And you, my friend, are the constant creator and operator of this never-ending Ferris wheel.

The pattern of thinking you are not valuable unless you are working, or not enough, or unlovable unless you are perfect pops its ugly head in your relationships, work, love, money, sex, spirituality, body image, and how to raise your family. And while you are busy running your life on empty, the pattern is strategically disqualifying you from new possibilities. "Who are you to change career paths now?" says the voice in your head.

The Paradox Pattern keeps you stuck in your circumstances, beholden to external validation, and too busy to go within your thoughts to uncover and reveal the most vibrant self inside of you. The embedded beliefs are limiting, to say the least, because you will only go as far as the Ferris wheel's circumference, never stretching beyond what is currently possible.

## MY CIRCUS, MY MONKEYS

"Not my circus, not my monkeys" is a Polish expression that means that your problem is not my problem. Thing is, your life is your circus, and these are your monkeys.

Let's take a look inside the Paradox Pattern of your mind when it's in action. Imagine you are the ringmaster of a traveling circus. You are the leader of your life, right?

Standing on a cracked stool in a worn red velvet jacket with golden tassel flourishes and top hat, you shout, "Welcome to the sideshow attraction known as my Paradox Pattern! Come one, come all, round and round on the carousel. Buy a ticket, peek inside a festival of bright pulsating lights, one-of-a-kind, never-before-seen thrillers, and cheap funnel cakes! Have I got a show for you!"

**IDENTIFYING YOUR PARADOX PATTERN**

"To my left, I have my cast of characters, the false identities I've carefully curated for your viewing pleasure. First up, we have the fire-eating muscle man in his vinyl crotch rocket briefs, ready to take on any slight of client criticism."

"The belly dancing snake charmer is here to woo you with her southern charm, and glittering excuses to get her way."

"Clients and co-workers, look on in amazement as the daring acrobat, teetering on the edge of a death-defining fall, gracefully leaps from one trapeze to the next, with an air of grace and control, praying not to miss the high bar and fall to her doom."

"To my right I have my side-kick monkey, always whispering in my ear, telling me what to do. It's as if he has puppet strings attached to my innermost thoughts."

"Together with my assemblage of quirky characters, my Paradox controls my every move."

"We've been practicing for years. Everyone has their costume on, makeup pressed, and wigs poofed. Agendas are micromanaged, and time is stretched down to the second. Each act thoughtfully overarticulated and orchestrated with a veil of tension that we think you cannot see. Places please, everyone!"

Have you ever felt like you have a circus running in your head? Let's make it real.

**FIND YOUR CLEAR VISION**

The greatest show on earth starts on a mundane Tuesday morning. You signal your snake charmer to woo your way through the first meeting with her hips twisting small gold coins which distract everyone just enough so you can get out of the meeting quickly. She takes her bow, and you race to your next meeting.

In between meetings your sidekick, the ever-present monkey, claps his rhythmic cymbals, ordering another social media post to inspire, educate, or entertain your followers. Done. Check. Move on.

Your day moves on like this, from one moment to the next, barely leaving time to go to the bathroom. And when you do, let's be real, you're on your phone.

For your final act, the grand finale, your inner fire-eating muscle man abuses his authoritative presence, asking co-workers to stay late to pick up the leftovers from the day's work.

At the end of the show, your boss applauds with a knowing smile that you've got everything under control. Little do they know that underneath the circus tent, you are teetering on the edge of a tightrope that could snap at any moment. Underneath the big tent, your audience would see it's all an illusion, a story of your own making, so the monkey continues to clap without pause.

## IDENTIFYING YOUR PARADOX PATTERN

Any break in the circus act and the whole thing would collapse, and you, as you have set up your life, would fall apart. And sometimes the illusion breaks.

He asks for a divorce.

Your job is eliminated.

Someone close to you dies unexpectedly.

You miscarry.

The world turns upside down in a global pandemic.

You're passed over for a big promotion.

You're too old.

Too young.

Too qualified.

Underqualified.

All of which confirms the pattern that you are not enough.

Contemporary corporate culture has taught us that we are paid for quantity over quality, for perfection over mistakes, and performance over learning. We are, in essence, paid to be in our Paradox Pattern, trapped in the societal, generational, and cultural expectations of what we are supposed to do, yet we are waking up to the realization that this isn't all it's cracked up to be—that the Ferris wheel of outdated expectations may be wrong, and that our comfort zone is, in fact, extremely uncomfortable.

We've been downplaying our true identity because it doesn't fit the mold, which only makes the Paradox Pattern stronger. Releasing the Paradox and blowing up how we are "supposed to do" life is a little scary because there is no roadmap. What if we trip, fall, or—*gasp*—lose control?

We have been taught to be scared of our full power as a fully expressed people.

"Don't bite off more than you can chew."

"Never show them what you are thinking."

"Pull yourself together."

So we hold tight to the limiting story, which at its core is self-contradictory, and once you take away the powerful storytelling that has been woven into our culture, the repetitive pattern doesn't have to be true for us. Not anymore.

The Paradox Pattern uses a classic disqualification strategy, stigmatizing you from the inside out, to keep your core limiting belief, that you are not enough, alive and kicking. Your Paradox Pattern keeps you at odds from dreaming too big, living too loud, or stepping fully into who you are meant to be.

## IDENTIFYING YOUR PARADOX PATTERN

Your Paradox has tools to limit your growth, exclude you from the crowd, and deem you unfit for happiness until you prove you are worthy of love and validation. It will weaken you, and disable and disbar your ideas before they come out of your mouth.

Its job is to keep you locked in an unconscious dropbox of limiting beliefs, thoughts, and feelings that stop you from seeing your future and being worthy of living your fullest expression.

A new future awaits you on the other side of your Paradox, but before you can get off the Ferris wheel and step into a brighter future, you need to take a look at what you got here in the first place.

You can't move forward towards your future vision with blind spots in your past.

Chapter 5

# MEET YOUR PARADOX PATTERN

YOU'RE PROBABLY GOING TO FEEL UNCOMFORTABLE IN this chapter, and you'll be tempted to skip it. Don't.

This chapter is going to reveal why you are stuck, why you can't change, and why you think you aren't worthy of being who you are truly meant to become. Once you "see" your pattern, you can't unsee it, and that's hard for some people because your identity has been tied to your Paradox Pattern. On the other hand, I have clients who meet their Paradox Pattern and erupt with joyous laughter because they finally see—"Oh yes! That's that thing I do!"

Here's why it's the most important part of the reinvention process: Without knowing your Paradox Pattern, you will stay stuck. Without exploring your shadow side, you'll never uncover the brilliant, vibrant you that is sparkling just below the surface, waiting to be seen.

## MEET YOUR PARADOX PATTERN

Societal, generational, and cultural expectations have crafted an identity of who you think you should be, and over time you've collected the thoughts, beliefs, and ideas of who you think you are. These thoughts and beliefs are your Ego.

"Hi, Ego!"

Maybe it's your parents' voice in your head that tells you:

"That's not how you do it."

"Don't fix what's not broken."

"Good girls don't do that."

"Get over yourself, you're not that special."

Maybe that was how it worked, for them, but it doesn't have to be true for you. Living inside of other people's expectations of how life should be doesn't leave room for creativity, curiosity, or building your future vision.

To expand your energy and trust yourself as you begin your Clear Vision journey, you have to build the self-awareness of what triggers your unconscious thoughts, opinions, and viewpoints. Otherwise, you continue to believe they are true.

Abraham-Hicks tells us that "a belief is only a thought you've been thinking." But what if the thoughts you've been thinking aren't true? What if they are just familiar patterns on repeat?

**FIND YOUR CLEAR VISION**

Your brain loves patterns. Patterns make life easier. After all, you don't have to think too hard about what to do because your brain has created neural pathways based on thoughts that lead to feelings that lead to action.

Because the Ego is based on thoughts and beliefs that you are not enough or unlovable, it spends a lot of time and energy trying to protect you from harm, hurt feelings, or breaking down completely. When you are triggered—let's say someone questions your opinion or your point of view, you receive harsh feedback framed as "creative criticism," or someone breaks up with you—your Paradox Pattern kicks into high alert.

A trigger can be as simple as someone at work glancing in your direction. Blood rises to your ears, and you feel your heart beating in your chest. Maybe you flush and start to think, "What was that look all about? Does she know something I don't? Did I do something? Does she not like me?" You are upset and not quite sure at what.

You begin to think, "I must have done something wrong, that's why she looked at me sideways."

Before you even know *why* she glanced your way, your brain has initiated the thought, "I'm unlovable because I must have done something wrong, and I have to be perfect in order to be loved."

The Paradox Pattern reinforces that you should be upset, which puts you on the perpetual Ferris wheel of frustration,

## MEET YOUR PARADOX PATTERN

unhappiness, and unwillingness to be open to new thoughts and ideas. Your Paradox Pattern spends a lot of time creating thoughts and feelings to prove it's right, which means that someone or something else has to be wrong. There is only one winner in this game: the Ego.

Your repetitive thoughts and feelings are a reminder that your Ego is alive and present. It's screaming and poking you with its claws to torture you with the thoughts "No one likes you. You aren't qualified to be here, just look at all the reasons why—there is too much to do, and you are never going to get ahead." Or "You're bored...this job is boring, you don't care, don't even think about giving it your all, the client is just going to change it all tomorrow anyway." This voice in your head has many names: your Ego, Monkey Mind, Lizard Brain, the Devil's Child. It's a tiny, small voice in your head that packs a big punch. It's an ass-backward way of "protecting" you from harm that is limiting your creativity, thoughts, and future.

Swiss philosopher and psychiatrist Carl Jung influenced the birth of ontology, the study of being. He believed there are universal patterns, habits, and memories that are common to all of mankind that account for how we show up in the world. According to Jung, our Persona is the mask we present. It's the version of us we let others see. Your Paradox Pattern is the thoughts, feelings, and actions that protect your Persona, in theory keeping up the appearance of the mask to protect you from harm or judgment from others.

## FIND YOUR CLEAR VISION

We learn at a young age to hide thoughts and feelings that may be out of what society or our close family think is the norm. We learn how to "act like a man" or "act like a woman," and if we don't confine ourselves to these patterns, our Ego makes us wrong for it, thus the loop begins to hide what isn't "right" about you. The Ego's work is to suppress feelings, creativity, and desires that we are told may be unsafe. It creates self-doubt and mistrust of our intuition and perceived shortcomings.

You've been giving your Ego too much power. The Ego loves to create separation so it can be right and justified in its thinking. Creating boundaries to survive and protect you from harm (thank you, Ego; that's very kind, but large four-legged animals are not chasing me through the African Sahara as of yet), it loves to have enemies, someone outside of yourself to blame for why things are the way they are. As you engage in a deeper, more purposeful relationship with your conscious thoughts and take actions from an elevated space, you raise the energetic vibrations of your thinking.

And guess what? You are rising.

Because—have you met yourself? You are a powerful, intelligent, and creative human being. You bring life to ideas, you create something out of nothing, you are loved and a lover. Yes, you! But, amazing you, you downplay you. You make yourself small. I imagine you thinking, "Lisa, this is nice and all, but it's not me. I'm just...insert there your small disqualification excuse for why you are not special."

### MEET YOUR PARADOX PATTERN

Notice how quickly our Paradox disqualifies a compliment? Self-awareness of your thoughts, feelings, and actions is a ticket off the Ferris wheel and into the Messy Middle towards your vision.

## PARADOX PATTERN WITHIN THE DRAMA TRIANGLE

The drama triangle is a popular psychological model of how dysfunctional our social and emotional interactions with others can be when we are coming from our Paradox Pattern. Each type of energy in the triangle—victim, abuser, and rescuer—has its own flavor of paradox. The triangle keeps us stuck inside of our repetitive patterns to, as Carl Jung would say, mask our fullest self, our desires, and our potential.

If the drama triangle is about how we interact with others, the Anti-Creator Consciousness is about how we interact and battle with ourselves. Anti-Creator Consciousness is the energy within each of us that plays the devil's advocate, and stops new ideas dead in their tracks. The battle commences within our mind, so not only are we masking our true self from others in the drama triangle, but we are also hiding our fullest potential from ourselves.

I'm going to share with you the distinctions between the drama triangle, Anti-Creator Consciousness, and individual Paradox Patterns within each model so you can see the pattern and how it's preventing you from your potential creativity ideas.

**FIND YOUR CLEAR VISION**

The Paradox Patterns are broken into active and passive expressions. An active expression is how you act when you feel wrong, attacked, or judged. A passive expression, or energy, is how you hold onto the feeling after the experience passes. Typically this is held in angry resentful energy or in dismissal or disdain towards yourself or others.

PSA: This is the hard part, this is where you will be triggered. You will think, "But I'm not a victim! I don't do that!" If you notice that type of reaction popping up for you, this is the opportunity to practice creating white space and to be with the thought a little bit longer. A trigger is a space to learn from, not run from.

Step into the discomfort of whatever may show up for you. This is your opportunity to gain massive self-awareness and pop out of thoughts you may have held as truth. Let's begin.

## PARADOX PATTERNS IN THE DRAMA TRIANGLE

### 1. Victim Energy in the Drama Triangle

The victim's primary fear is that they are unlovable and not enough, which expresses itself in different ways. When the victim feels wronged, they see life through a lens of constant defeat and lack of control.

"Poor me, there's nothing I can do about this because these things always happen to me."

## MEET YOUR PARADOX PATTERN

Be careful playing the victim, because your story of "never being able to catch a break" will manifest itself through sub-par opportunities, proving to yourself that you are a victim. The victim will apply for jobs they don't want and don't receive calls back for, justifying they never get what they want.

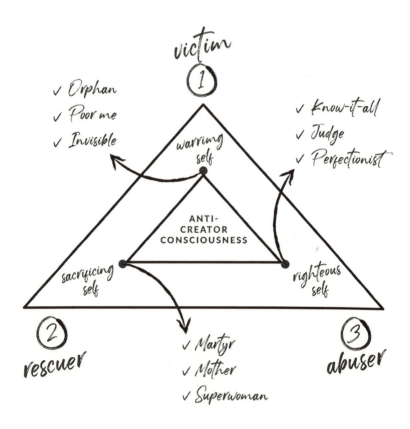

The victim role takes it a step further and armors itself with layers of self-protection to avoid getting hurt. Inside this layer, the victim becomes the Warring Self. The Victim begins to use their voice for jealousy, gossip, and to block those who don't align with their thoughts. This helps them stay stuck in "these things always happen to me" and to recruit others into the story. "See? I told you—these things always happen to me. Did you hear what so-and-so said about me?"

It's a self-fulling inner battle of distrust, disconnection, and a game plan to avoid potential pain. What's missing for the Victim and the Warring Self is any sense of connection to themselves or others.

### *Archetypal Paradox Patterns within Victim Energy*

*Orphan Paradox Pattern*

The Orphan fears that they are unlovable or that they will be left behind because they did something bad or wrong. The Orphan overcompensates by seeking attention and people-pleasing. This is actively expressed through neediness and passively expressed, or held onto, as lonely inner child energy.

*Poor Me Paradox Pattern*

Poor Me's greatest fear is that they are not enough, and they overcompensate by seeking validation and gathering stories to prove they are always the victim. This energy actively expresses itself when they gather evidence that "bad things always happen to me, see?" It passively shows up in fear, hiding, and a limited outlook on life.

*Invisible Paradox Pattern*

Invisible's greatest fear is that someone will discover that they are not enough. They overcompensate by hiding so people can't see the "real me." Their passive, ongoing energy is often rooted in shame and the feeling that it's selfish to stand out. Actively they tell others that they are shy, introverted, and humble so people will leave them alone in their pattern of hiding.

## 2. Rescuer Energy in the Drama Triangle

The Rescuer always has time for others, helping everyone around them but themselves. The "office mom" is an example of this energy. For all you people-pleasers out there doing other people favors, gosh, that's very sweet of you, but does it leave you depleted with little to no energy for yourself? What are you avoiding in yourself by helping others all the time?

When the Rescuer role embeds into the Anti-Creator Consciousness, they become the Sacrificing Self. A constant martyr or a sacrificial lamb, there is no room for themselves. It's a tight loop of serving others, and any feeling of creativity, love, or joy for themselves is seen as selfish. They are riddled with shame, guilt, and remorse for not doing more. Women have been pinged as the caretaker and shamed if they do not live up to society's standards of what it means to take care of everyone. It's no wonder the Sacrificing Self runs strong and deep into our collective psyche of what a woman should and should not be doing. What's missing for the Rescuer and Sacrificing Self is self-love and acceptance that you are valuable outside of helping others.

### *Archetypal Paradox Patterns within Rescuer Energy*

### *Martyr Paradox Pattern*

The Martyr's greatest fear is that they are a burden. Their pattern is to sacrifice their happiness, wellbeing, and time by "doing it all." It's hard to argue with a martyr because this pattern shows up under the veil of being a healer, or do-gooder, and expresses itself taking care of everyone else because they are the only ones who know how to. Passively, this energy shows up as brokenness and saviorism.

### *Mother Paradox Pattern*

Mother's greatest fear is that they are unlovable. The Mother's strategy is to take care of and provide comfort to everyone, because once everyone is happy, then they will be happy, but not a moment before. This pattern actively expresses itself as a frazzled and overwhelmed person with no time for themselves, and passively shows up as guilt, shame, and blame.

*Superwoman Paradox Pattern*

Superwoman's greatest fear is that they are weak and vulnerable, so their strategy is to fly in and save the day, to prove they are strong, even if no one needs saving. Actively this pattern shows up as hero energy, and passively it shows up as not wanting to show any sign of weakness, vulnerability, or suffering.

### 3. Abuser Energy in the Drama Triangle

And finally, the bully of the group, the abuser who is never wrong and is always overcompensating to prove to others that they are always right.

The abuse can show up as misogyny, sexism, and racism or may show up in subtle microaggressions and gaslighting. The worst abuser of them all is the one in your head bullying you to believe that only *your* logic is logical: "It's us against them!"

The final corner of the Anti-Creator Consciousness Triangle is the Righteous Self. The abuser has become so binary in its thinking and doing that life has become black and white. It's impossible to connect to others or themselves because they spend all of their energy convincing others and themselves that they are right. Their inner world is filled with disdain, which leaves feelings of grief and defeat. What's missing is calm, peace, and any space for understanding.

## Archetypal Paradox Patterns within Abuser Energy

### Know-It-All Paradox Pattern

The Known-It-All's greatest fear is that they are only enough if they can control all the circumstances around them. So their pattern is to take control of the situation. This is actively expressed by being a know-it-all, always being the leader, self-serving outbursts, and making everything "all about what's most important to me." Its passive expression is seen as a lack of vulnerability and fear of surrendering to the unknown.

### The Judge Paradox Pattern

The Judge's greatest fear is that they are wrong, so their strategy is to always be right and fight to prove it. The Judge's energy expresses itself as "Me versus the world! Never surrender!" and passively expresses as closed off and alone.

## MEET YOUR PARADOX PATTERN

*Perfectionist Paradox Pattern*

This is where I spent my time, in the dropbox of perfection to prove I was valuable. Perfectionists' greatest fear is that someone will think we are weak. Actively this shows up as rumination, overcompensation, and constant polishing. Passively, perfectionism shows up as imposter syndrome; and, to us, vulnerability is considered a sign of weakness.

Your Paradox Pattern leaves little room for white space because you are constantly overcompensating to prove you are valuable, lovable, or enough, which leads to frustration, anger, and burnout. This is classic emotional unavailability as you are blocked, stuck, or completely closed off to thoughts and feelings outside of your pattern. When you are stuck, your Clear Vision hits the brakes, and not surprisingly you find yourself thinking, "Who in the world am I?"

When your Paradox is running the show, you're disconnected from your most true and vibrant self.

Hey, listen, I've taken on every one of these archetypes in my life.

When my kids get on my nerves, Poor Me says, "I never get any alone time!"

My Superwoman sometimes tells my husband, "I can sense you're stressed because of work. Don't worry, I'll go to the

**FIND YOUR CLEAR VISION**

store, get dinner, do the dishes, put the kids to bed, and then work on my business. Don't worry, I've got all of this handled."

I've also played the Know-It-All, mostly with myself. I try to control everything to feel like I have a sense of normalcy while the world is upside down when, in reality, pretending to know it all leaves me depleted and in an overly masculine energy vibration—which inevitably attracts more masculine energy—so I try to control things more.

Ridiculous cycle when you take a deep look, right?

The inner layers of the drama triangle, the Anti-Creator Consciousness, and Archetypical Paradox Patterns allow you to witness who you are being so you can choose outside of the story you have believed to be true for so long.

So how do you unhook from these powerful anchors in your consciousness?

Especially when we love a juicy drama-filled reality show?

Especially when it's easier to blame others rather than trust ourselves?

Inner trust is practiced in the white space between your default paradoxical reaction and a new choice. Building a relationship with inner trust becomes one in vulnerability and faith that you've got this.

## MEET YOUR PARADOX PATTERN

Your Paradox will go wild. Surrendering to inner trust is not in alignment with taking action from a place of righteousness. Surrender is a triggering word for many. What about you? What comes to mind when I say the word "surrender?" What about grace? Weakness, or vulnerability? That means you aren't perfect, right? That you probably messed up, right? Notice what type of energy you are plugged into when you feel like you have to surrender the sacrificing, warring, or righteous energy.

What's that energy covering up for you? Look right underneath your default energy to see what emotion is underneath.

You desire peace over conflict, but your warring self won't hear of it.

You desire grace over perfection, but your righteous self won't allow it.

You desire to trust yourself, but your sacrificing self won't open up enough to let it in.

## WHAT GOT YOU TO WHERE YOU ARE TODAY WON'T GET YOU TO WHERE YOU WANT TO GO

Here's the catch. What you spend a large amount of time on now is what is going to keep you stuck in the dropbox and disconnected from your Clear Vision. Your Paradox is looking for ways to keep you doing what you are good at to prove it's true. Your Paradox is perfectly happy being known for your current title or current business model. But your heart and soul desire more.

You can't reinvent your life by doing. Reinvention comes from who you are being. I get it. You're just too damn busy organizing, controlling, and taking responsibility for everything. What are you so busy doing that's worth you missing out on who you want to become?

When do you just get to be enough? When is enough, enough? I don't agree with the self-help rhetoric of "being enough." Where's that barometer? Who holds the scale for enough and why are we being measured against it?

What if we are simply done?

I'm done.

I'm done being a mirror for society's fantasy. I'm done being a reflection of the judgments of what I should or should not be. I'm done being too much of anything. Too much sugar, spice, and everything nice. My future is filled with a funky fresh fire. With a flaming source of energy that runs through my core, shining down from the heavens, rooted into the earth, with a knowing that is deep, bold, daring, flamboyant, and strong.

## MEET YOUR PARADOX PATTERN

Yes, you can be all of it. It's your rodeo, my dear. You ride that bull however your heart desires. This is the ah-ha "that's why I do that thing!" moment you have been waiting for. Your queendom has come. You are ready to pop and move into what's truly possible for you.

Welcome to the other side of your Paradox. Now you're ready for the real work: Making choices. Choosing outside of what's predictable for you, beyond the dropbox of your Paradox and popping into your Clear Vision. But in order to get there, we have to go through the Messy Middle.

When you are stuck in the repetitive cycle of your Paradox, it's as if you are in a box, bouncing back and forth, looping between self-doubt, self-righteousness, and frustration. Interestingly enough, if you simply look up, tilt your chin away from your phone, and the Excel file of to-dos, you'll notice your box is open.

This is the Paradox. Your box of confusion, "must-do's," and "no ways" is wide open, and you can get out of it anytime. In fact, when you pop your head up and look around, you are closer to your Clear Vision than ever before.

## FIND YOUR CLEAR VISION

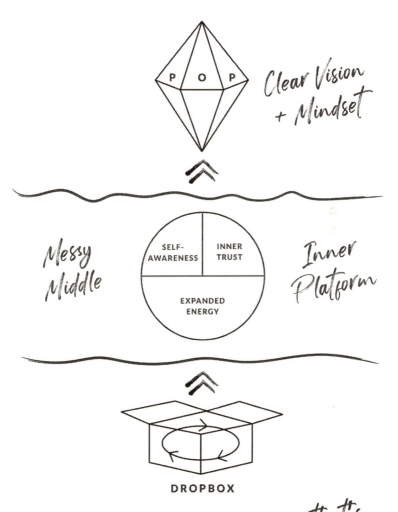

## MEET YOUR PARADOX PATTERN

## IT'S THE PARADOX OF CHOICE: POP OR DROP

Here's a quick way to frame a dropbox thought to a pop thought.

### Dropbox Thought: Have. Do. Be.

I have to (do something), then I'll be (insert the desired feeling).

I have to take care of everyone else, then I'll be happy.

I have to work hard, then I'll be successful.

I have to lose weight, get a spray tan, Botox, a haircut and color, and a new hobby, then I'll find a boyfriend and be happy.

You can add lots of things to accomplish in front of the desired emotion you really want; that's a great way to constantly postpone how you want to feel.

### Pop Thought: Be. Do. Have.

When I am (insert the desired feeling), I can (do something) and have (what you really desire to do).

When I'm being creative, I can come up with lots of new ideas and have fun.

## FIND YOUR CLEAR VISION

When I'm being open, I can be on a blind date and have a great time.

When I'm being focused, I can finish my work quickly and have time with the kids.

Now, I'm not saying it will be a one-and-done, you don't pop out of the dropbox, and boom that's the end of your self-awareness work. Choosing your thoughts is a daily, moment-by-moment practice. And, at first, choosing outside of what's predictable for you will land you squarely in the Messy Middle, a land of uncertainty, and sometimes, quite frankly, discomfort.

And guess what? Great news! Now we know what's been keeping you stuck: your fear of being uncomfortable.

The Messy Middle is a place where you don't know the answers, where you aren't always right, and where you'll want to overthink everything. But it's also the gateway between today and what is currently impossible—living your life by design.

I want you to pause for a moment. Take a deep inhale and exhale.

One.

Two.

## MEET YOUR PARADOX PATTERN

Close your eyes and ask your vibrant future self, the version of you that's spending most of their time in the pop, "What does it feel like to be me?"

Safe. Worthy. Wise. Creative. Aligned. Connected. Brave. Bold.

What feelings are you filled with when you trust that your vibrant future self has your back? Add texture and color to that feeling. What does that feeling look like, smell like, or feel like? Make it real.

When I asked my client, the VP of brand strategy at a Fortune 500 company, he said, "Being me feels like clarity. It's an iridescent highway. There's no doubt that it's the right path for me. It's a sound bath of meditative beats that keep my heart and brain connected. It smells like a warm spring morning right after the sun has risen."

He painted a clear picture of what it looks, sounds, and feels like to trust that his future self is a trustworthy ally in his Clear Vision journey. Painting a picture by engaging your five senses—the picture of you being your most vibrant self—will help you pop when your Paradox wants you to drop.

In between the pop and drop is the Messy Middle. Don't worry, I'll share the exact framework to create your Inner Platform to support you as you move through this part of your journey. Let's define the first of four pillars of your Inner Platform, your Clear Vision.

**FIND YOUR CLEAR VISION**

Let's agree that the dropbox is done. We are willing to be in the Messy Middle and play a new game, one where we create the rules, and we know how to win. We're creating your life by design.

> **BRIGHT TOOL:**
> **YOUR PARADOX PATTERN'S MANIFESTO**
>
> Here are a few questions to provoke your pattern on purpose. Journal for one to two minutes on each of these questions. It's a quick brain dump, from your Ego, so let it rip. It doesn't have to be good, realistic, or logical. No one else is going to read this except you.

These will help you fill in the blank for your Paradox Pattern Manifesto.

1. Think back to when you were between the ages of five to eight years old. When was the first time you felt that you were not enough, wrong, or unlovable? What happened?

2. What did that experience teach you you had to be to avoid feeling like that? Use the sentence stem: "It taught me that I had to be (fill in the blank)."

3. Now, as an adult, what actions do you take to make sure that feeling doesn't pop up again?

## MEET YOUR PARADOX PATTERN

4. As an adult, if you keep doing those actions, to avoid feeling that way, you think you will be:

- Loved

- Perfect

- Enough

- Included

- Smart enough

- Good enough

- Special

- Accepted

- Desired

- Valuable

Or, if you don't keep doing those actions you think you will be:

- Stupid

- Unlovable

- Unworthy

# FIND YOUR CLEAR VISION

- Not enough

- Excluded

- Unwanted

Your Paradox Pattern: "**I have to be** (feeling from #2) **in order to be** (feeling from #4)"

**I have to be** perfect **in order to be** loved.

The final step is to create a Paradox Manifesto.

"I have to be _____ in order to be _____."

Or try wording it like this:

I have to _____ to prove I'm _____.

I have to _____ so I don't look _____.

I have to _____ so no one sees that I am _____.

Download all of the Paradox Patterns and a blank Paradox Pattern Manifesto at: www.bebrightlisa.com/findyourclearvision-book

Now that you have uncovered the blind spots in your thinking by identifying your Archetypical Paradox Pattern and its manifesto, it's time to build your Clear Vision.

## Chapter 6

# BUILD YOUR CLEAR VISION

My client Stevie started our coaching session, telling me she wanted to find her purpose. Then she shared all the things she had done in her life, quite successfully, while looking for her purpose. She was a successful lawyer who had always been at the top of her class in school. She had three beautiful children and a loving husband who was also a professional.

She checked all the boxes on her career path and created a good family life. She was, by all means, happy. But she felt she was being called to create something greater than herself. In her school and career path, there was always the next step to take. Having been told what to do to be successful most of her life left her feeling stuck and lost because she didn't know what to do anymore. Without a final destination, she felt dead in her tracks.

## BUILD YOUR CLEAR VISION

Oftentimes, without knowing the final destination, which is a symptom of the Paradox, we feel stuck because the Paradox doesn't have a box to check off and declare, "I've found my purpose! There it is. Let's move on."

Here's what was happening. Stevie had popped up into the Messy Middle. She knew something was out there, but she was afraid to play in this new space because she thought she needed to hold tightly to the rigidity of the awards and professional accomplishments to be successful. She said the things she could check off were the things she judged her life by. Outside of the dropbox is a future that has not yet happened; it's not a tangible piece of paper, or a degree, a certification, or a skill set. It's not a physical location…yet. It's a vision of the future, a blank canvas to design.

Our Paradox will have us making assumptions that this can't be true—our future isn't blank! Instead, it will have us over-preparing with details, data, and research, to prove that we need a final destination. We need to do something, but we just don't know what that thing is. So we get frustrated and give up.

"Tell me more about this calling. What do you want to create?" I asked her.

"Whenever somebody asks me, I go blank. I don't know. Literally, a blank wall appears in front of me, and I can't see around it," she replied.

## FIND YOUR CLEAR VISION

The first response always comes from the dropbox, so I took a different angle. "Imagine that you are looking at that blank wall right now, and you can just let it be there. Maybe, just for a moment, you can see through it, or peek around the side, or over the top. Let's imagine you can see through it, even though it's fuzzy. Let's just go around it, for just a moment. How do you feel on the other side?"

She paused, and said, "It's peaceful on the other side. I feel present."

She went on to say that she no longer felt self-doubt. And in fact, she felt confident. She said on the other side of the blank wall, she could show up as her full self with love and a sense of curiosity. Now that she was connected to what may be possible on the other side of "not knowing," I asked her to elevate a little more. "Imagine that you are being all of those things. You're being your full self, showing up authentically, with presence, love, and curiosity. What are you doing when you're being that way?"

She was quiet for a few moments and then said, "I'm spending a lot of time collaborating and in community with other business owners. I'm developing a shared co-working space for lawyers, accountants, photographers, people who need space to connect with clients, a space that is good looking—not just an afterthought with coffee stains on the beige conference room table."

**BUILD YOUR CLEAR VISION**

Now that her imagination was flowing, she said she would be creating a women's weekend, somewhere that women could connect and collaborate.

I took it further and elevated the question from her business ideas into her personal life.

"What about in your personal life or at home? If you were being this way, what would you be doing there?"

Again, the idea of space popped up. She said that she would have more personal space and take up a hobby, like painting. She continued to explore and said she would redecorate her home with brighter colors. She and her husband had been living there for six years, and always talked about redecorating but never made it a priority. It's interesting what you can live with for so long—that 1960's dark wood paneling and those forest green walls become the norm.

In her personal relationships, she wanted to spend more time with her husband. They had spent most of their married life working on their professional careers and raising children, which left little time for them to stay connected.

As she was playing with the possibilities beyond the blank wall, just for fun, she threw in a sauna in the backyard because—why not? Her most vibrant self wants to have fun, dream, play, and create possibilities…because it can.

**FIND YOUR CLEAR VISION**

I noticed an overarching theme, or what we call a concept in the design world, which unified the idea behind the message from her vibrant self, which she was open to receiving: Space. Space to breathe, collaborate, and connect. She desired space to build community. Likewise, in her personal life, she desired space to slow down and create an environment reflective of the peace, calm, and connection she desired.

Concepts are ideas that encompass the message, metaphor, or thought that a designer wants the viewer to feel and be led by in their design. It's not even something you can really touch or grab on to. Space, as it relates to Stevie's vision, could be a physical location, space within her heart, or even space between each breath.

I took her back to the beginning of our conversation. "How did you create space for yourself while you were checking off all the boxes of success?" I asked.

"I didn't. I didn't have space for myself. I was doing things for my family or my clients. I was helping them create a better life, but rarely did I take even a breath or a pause for myself to give myself space."

"Why's that?"

"I thought that in order to be successful I had to take care of everyone else first, which didn't leave space for me." Classic Martyr Paradox.

## BUILD YOUR CLEAR VISION

Her Paradox Pattern had her walking in circles behind a blank wall of not knowing her purpose because she was so busy taking care of everyone else. Oftentimes, the thing we most desire is the thing we give to everyone else.

This pattern is especially true for women who carry the stereotype of being caretakers, people-pleasers, and believe that to do otherwise would be selfish. Your wellbeing isn't even on the to-do list, which keeps you walking in circles behind a blank wall of stuck.

For so long you have been doing what you are told, whether by your boss, society, or even that small inner voice in your head soaked in stereotypes. Now is the time to reclaim what is rightfully yours: a vision that shines out your highest and best. A Clear Vision—even better, imagine it's a disco ball—to reflect your talents and gifts from the inside out that will make your heart sing and, yes, be done with ease, enjoyment, and pleasure.

When you shift from the drop to the pop and embody how you want to see your future—from a place of clarity and purpose, one that is based in who you are, followed by what you are doing—it can be fun and creative. And you can be that way today.

In our next session I asked her, "How do you feel now that you are willing to stay in the Messy Middle?"

"Now that I'm in the Messy Middle, I find so much joy in getting curious about what feels good to me and to pop into my true self—it's DELIGHTFUL to surprise myself. When I think about creating more space in my life, I feel like a little kid splashing in mud puddles on the way home from school."

Can you imagine a vision of your life that is so rich it gives you pleasure to create? Hell, it may even make you want to dance outside in the rain!

It's a new game that we have not been playing because we've spent so long trying to fit into the paradoxical box of the cultural cardboard construct of a patriarchal world.

Unlike the Paradox Pattern, your Clear Vision is a winnable game because it's your new mindset that you dream and manifest. It's the game of reinvention, a declaration of what's important, and who you need to be to create it. It's rooted in legit and long-lasting goals. By nature, it's creative because you are living and breathing it every day, and celebrating the journey of making your vision a reality.

Unlike your life's purpose or "following your passion," as popular culture would lead you to believe is the be-all and end-all, your Clear Vision isn't based on accomplishments or productivity. Rather, it's a new mindset based on what creates genuine happiness for you, and how you and your gifts can contribute to the world.

Let's be real. Making a long-lasting sustainable transformation of your life by design is going to challenge you to your core. It's asking you to give up stories that have been holding

## BUILD YOUR CLEAR VISION

you in the same pattern of being stuck for decades. But that doesn't make it impossible. Your Clear Vision is supported by your Inner Platform that is surrounded by inner trust, self-awareness, and a clear mindset. Sustainable transformation is possible and powerful because personal creative power is when you declare something possible and make it a reality. Let's make what was impossible to see possible.

## CLEAR VISION FRAMEWORK

### Clear Vision Components

CLEAR is an acronym that stands for:

**C**lear Concept

**L**egit and Long-lasting

**E**xpanded Energy

**A**spirational Success

**R**ooted In Celebration

Your Clear Vision is contained within a declaration, an affirmation of what you are creating, why it's important, and who you need to be to bring it to life. It is how you plan to create your future by design. It's a pop thought: Be. Do. Have. With a strategy.

## Clear Vision Declaration

*I am here to* _____

*and this is important because* _____

*I will* _____

*and the first step is to* _____

*Starting today I am being* _____

*Success looks like* _____

*I will celebrate by* _____

(Download a blank Clear Vision Declaration at: www.bebrightlisa.com/findyourclearvision-book)

It's an acknowledgment of who you are becoming, the experience of life you want to create, and how to do it. It's the culmination of who you want to be and what you want to do. This statement alone will give you radical agency over your life's outcomes.

A Clear Vision can be applied to any area of your life, career, business, spirituality, wellbeing, or leadership. Here are some examples:

## BUILD YOUR CLEAR VISION

**Thought Leadership:** Andi declared her article about millennial leadership would be published by *The Cut* before the new year.

**Career:** Dominic declared his Clear Vision was to set up virtual coffee dates with potential mentors from international teams to help him grow his executive presence.

**Community:** Lauren declared to grow her women's community to 5,000 people.

**Wellbeing:** Dinorah declared to eat a plant-based diet for three months.

**Creativity:** Aparna declared to perform her traditional Indian dancing at three venues.

**Spirituality:** Madeline declared to build an altar in her home for daily meditation.

**Entrepreneurship:** Carter declared to quit her job and become a creative leadership coach.

Listen, you can make all the money you want, and be wildly successful doing it, and simultaneously have fun and be breathless with love and energy every damn day. You just need to massively recalibrate the story you are telling yourself about what's possible for you.

The trick is to declare how you want to feel and to create a new story from pop thoughts. This is creativity at its core.

Designers, architects, painters, and poets see something that doesn't exist yet, and they make it real. Lingering in the space of the Messy Middle, and allowing yourself the wiggle room to feel safe, open, and connected to your Clear Vision will expand your energy and begin to connect your idea to reality.

## CLEAR STEP 1: CLEAR CONCEPT

> *Clear Concept: "I am here to...and this is important because..."*

When a creative team is given a client brief to kick off a project, their first step is to conceptualize ideas. A concept is the core idea, intention, and essence of your Clear Vision—in other words, the foundation on which your Clear Vision declaration is built.

Typically, designers will land on three concepts and start to sketch out the idea using visuals like a website design, an advertisement, or an editorial for a magazine, for example. Brainstorming is how you see if the idea has legs and will be strong enough to carry the concept through the design to make an impact. It's messy. It's wild and invigorating. And it can be fun if you let it.

After preparing rough sketches and layouts that detail the conceptual direction, designers think, "Okay, this may work," and start to apply design elements like typography, photography, illustration, and other stylizations that will make the

## BUILD YOUR CLEAR VISION

design come alive. Nothing is set in stone, but the vision is starting to take shape.

While creating your Clear Vision, you are both the designer and the client. You are going to brainstorm concepts and ideas for your Clear Vision.

Our new game is to dream up ideas and make them real. It means dreaming, exploring, discovering, and adventuring, then moving that vision into reality.

Finding and nurturing the concept behind your vision is pivotal. Your concept could be as big as space, human empowerment, affordable health and wellness, or an all-encompassing community. It could be as small and impactful as a new friendship, a deep connection to yourself, or a love match. It could be reinventing your relationship with food, your partner, your wellbeing, or your work. It's your vision, and it's what is right for you, right now.

The first step is to be in the right mindset to create by granting time and space for your most vibrant self to thrive. This means giving your Paradox the backseat. To awaken your vibrant self, we are going to create an environment for fun and mistakes. Get your favorite cup of tea, soda, coffee, bubbly La Croix, or something to stay hydrated and tickle your brain with liquid pleasure, because you're going to need the lubrication.

Take out a pen and paper—we're about to get messy.

## FIND YOUR CLEAR VISION

The brainstorming stage of the conceptual process is messy and disheveled, which is a good thing. We are going to sketch, draw, type, toss out, and reimagine until something rises to the surface of the pages of misspelled inner dialogue in your analog or digital journal. When your concept begins to surface, you are going to feel it in your bones, your body, your heart, and your soul. If you don't, start again. No one is rushing you but you. I invite you to slow down in order to speed up later.

Spend about thirty minutes brainstorming on the questions below, or take each question one by one to explore over a few days. This is your time, so covet it as sacred.

Keep your pen, pencil, or fingers moving the whole time. Just keep moving, writing, and receiving ideas from your bright brain onto paper. You may also find using a voice recorder helps you to stay in the flow of ideas. I auto dictate blog posts and even conceptual ideas for chapters in this book, using the voice memo on my phone.

Do what works for you to keep ideas flowing. We don't need to know how to execute the ideas; we just need to capture them.

Ready?

Take a few deep breaths.

One.

Two.

**BUILD YOUR CLEAR VISION**

Roll your shoulders up, down, and backward a few times. Continue to take big inhales and exhales as you roll any tension out of your neck and shoulders; you don't need to take into this practice any energy that isn't serving you. Exhale out anything that doesn't need to be with you on this journey. Give yourself these moments to explore.

Affirm to yourself: "I am the creator of my life. I am safe to explore what I most desire. I am here to listen, receive, and play."

## Step 1: Brainstorm

Read through these questions, then close your eyes for a few moments to ponder them. Closing your eyes signals to your subconscious that it is safe to rest and pause. Closing your eyes allows the brain to divert attention from your environment and instead focus on your inner world.

These questions may all lead to the same answer, or they may spark different ones. Just let whatever question resonates with you the most take the lead.

It may help to add a timeframe around the questions—like this year, next year, in the next six months, or in five years...it's your vision, so do what your heart desires.

Ask yourself:

**What do people ask me for advice on?**

This is going to reflect what you are currently known for in your business, career, or livelihood. It's what you are good at and may already be getting paid to do.

**What conversations do I want to be a part of in the future?**

This question will spark what you want to learn about and the direction in which you want to go.

**What do I want to spend more time doing that makes me feel alive?**

This will highlight what your vibrant self needs in order to pop, or it could be a future occupation. Gay Hendricks, author of *The Big Leap*, would say that this is your zone of genius, "where creativity flows freely and you are actively pursuing the things that offer you fulfillment and satisfaction."

**What do most people think is true, but I know there's another way to think about it?**

This is your difference maker and your thought leadership. You may think this is something that comes easy for you, and that's a good thing! Just because something comes easy for you doesn't mean it does for others. They want to see the world through your unique point of view.

## BUILD YOUR CLEAR VISION

**When I'm living my life from my Clear Vision, what does my day look like?**

Visualize your ideal day from the moment you wake up to the moment you lay down to rest. What types of activities are you doing and how do you feel throughout the day?

Take a few deep breaths and sit quietly, even if nothing is popping to the surface for you. Get curious about what does or doesn't arise. Breathe into the pause, stay in the Messy Middle. It's okay to feel fear or self-doubt, and it's okay not to know how you are going to do it. Facing your future may be overwhelming because you don't know how it's all going to happen, so simply be with your feelings and allow them to pass through your mind. You could write them down on a separate piece of paper so they have somewhere to go, then lay them aside and continue to brainstorm.

Get back to the brainstorming by writing down your thoughts, even the ones that don't make sense. Even if it's a grocery item you forgot to pick up yesterday; that's just your conscious mind releasing the day. Release all of the "stuff" and again, be with the Messy Middle and keep your pen on the page.

Write down whatever words, ideas, dreams, and thoughts you are being compelled to explore. I encourage you to keep writing for thirty minutes. It may seem like an eternity, or it may fly by in a heartbeat. Give yourself thirty minutes of brainstorming time; you are worth it.

To add to your brainstorming experience, we are going to ask questions that originated in Japan between 794 and 1185 A.D. The Japanese philosophy of the Ikigai (pronounced ee-kee-guy) helps people find purpose in their life, and the same questions can be applied to build your Clear Vision. Let's see how we can use its structure to deepen your Clear Vision brainstorm.

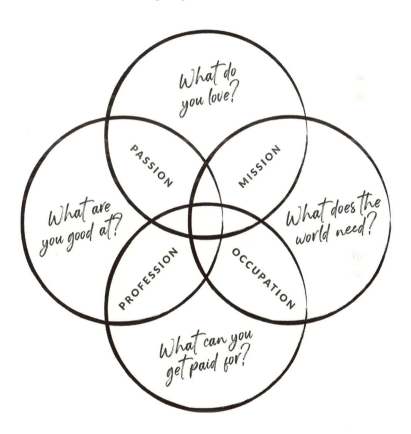

(Download a blank Ikigai diagram at: www.bebrightlisa.com/findyourclearvision-book)

**BUILD YOUR CLEAR VISION**

The Ikigai is set up in four overlapping circles that represent four areas of your life; it's a fantastic approach to the holistic whole-self strategy embodying your:

Passion

Mission

Occupation

Profession

When you overlap these four areas of life, you can see patterns that arise from blending what you love to do, your passion, with what you are good at, your profession. Then adding in what you can get paid for, your occupation, and what the world needs, the unique flavor of your gifts and ideas, will rise to the top of your mind, including ideas you never even knew were there. These questions will awaken things you may not have thought of before, maybe even things you have been taking for granted.

I led my Clear Vision U members through the Ikigai process. Tori, an alum of Clear Vision U, spent her career in law but was ready to move on. After brainstorming ideas for each of the four Ikigai questions, she realized that she's good at planning parties for charities; in fact, that weekend she was having thirty women over to her house for a fundraising party to support the local domestic violence shelter. What the Ikigai revealed was that she was passionate about charity work. Her time, energy, and intentions were all there and it was what the world needed, but she wasn't getting paid for it. It was a light-bulb moment that her next career move could be into fundraising for the causes she loves. Take another fifteen minutes or so to brainstorm the answers to these questions.

*Ikigai Questions*

**What do you love?** (Your passion)

**What are you good at?** (Your profession)

**What does the world need?** (Your mission)

**What can you get paid for?** (Your occupation)

## Step 2: Focus

Quickly release inner judgment by being unattached from any feelings of not knowing how to create what you just wrote down or feelings like "I can't do that!" which may have popped up. Now, read what you wrote for all of the questions. Are there any things you wrote that you feel like you should do, but, if you were being honest, you don't want to? Or do they sound really boring?

Cross them out. Throw them away; we don't need "shoulds" or ideas that are going to bore you in six months.

## BUILD YOUR CLEAR VISION

My client wrote down that she wanted to get her MCC, Masters in Coaching Certification from the International Coaching Federation, because that was the next step in moving up the proverbial ladder of her coaching career. But, if she was being honest, it didn't excite her to think about going through the process, and in fact, there were lots of other ideas that did light her up, so that idea got crossed off.

Another client wrote down that she wanted to get her inbox to zero. I asked, "Is that the problem that makes you feel alive?" "No"—the answer to that question was absolutely not. You can simply mark your emails as "read" and boom, problem solved.

Notice any to-do's that may have snuck onto your list. We are not here to solve problems that we already know how to solve. These "problems" are in the way of you preparing to create your Clear Vision. All of the thoughts that block you from your Clear Vision are your Paradox Pattern trying to grab your ankles and pull you back into the dropbox. Cross them out.

If it doesn't light you up, cross it out.

If it's something your mother or father wants you to do…and you don't, cross it out.

If it's something you feel you should do, but if you were being honest, you don't want to, cross it out.

If it's boring you, cross it out.

If you are unsure if you should cross it out or not, flip a coin. Seriously.

Heads you keep it, tails you cross it out. Flip a coin and notice the feeling that rises when it pops up. Were you relieved? Disappointed? The feeling is your most vibrant self giving you a clear signal of what it wants to do. Now follow it.

## Step 3: Elevate

**If there were no limits, what would you do?**

Does this spark any new ideas? Write them down.

If you removed all the barriers, all the "why not" and "who am I?", what would you do?

Now look at your delightful messy list and see if there is an idea that gives you butterflies. Or makes you feel warm inside, or scares you a little and gives you goosebumps (the good kind).

This is your vibrant self giving you another sign, so listen up! Take out a bright highlighter and highlight it!

Now you are going to review your list and begin to highlight the thoughts and ideas you think have a possibility for them. Begin to look for patterns in what you wrote down as well.

**BUILD YOUR CLEAR VISION**

As you move through the Ikigai, you can start to take the overarching thoughts and ideas and pop them into the Venn diagram, select a few words from each question, and put them into the corresponding areas. Once you have added the ideas to each circle, look to see if there is yet another pattern or idea rising to the surface. Notice what ideas are overlapping inside the circles. What ideas arise from "what the world needs" and "what you love"? Put that into the space labeled Mission. And continue to pull out the underlying ideas and concepts that correspond with each area of the Ikigai.

Now, if you are starting to sense an intention that is awakening an "oh, maybe that's something to explore!", then you are ready to move forward.

Or, if you are still in the Messy Middle, cool. Stay there. Pick your top three ideas, patterns, theories, or concepts that are floating to the top of your mind. These could be wildly different or be in the same general family. You're going to see if these ideas have legs and try them on for size in real life. In design, we call this "prototyping the idea" to see if it will work, and it's okay to have more than one at this stage; it's an opportunity to try on the concept.

### Step 4: Importance

The final question in the brainstorming process is the most important because it's what is going to get you through the moments when life is hard, you don't want to go on, and start thinking "wouldn't it just be easier to go back to my normal 9-5 job?"

**Why is this important?**

Stacey Abrams, an American politician, lawyer, voting rights activist, and author, shared three questions she asks herself about everything she does:

"What do I want?"

"Why do I want it?"

"How do I get it?"

Stacey says, "Figure out what the 'why' is for you, because jumping from the 'what' to the 'do' is meaningless if you don't know why. Because when it gets hard, when it gets tough, when your friends walk away from you, when your supporters forget you, when you don't win your first race—if you don't know why, you can't try again."

Knowing why this concept is important to you will keep you laser-focused and committed to creating it. Even when the outcome looks hazy or life gets in the way, it will become an inner mantra and saving grace to keep you motivated to design your Clear Vision each and every day.

**Clear Concept sentence stem:**

**"I am here to...and this is important because..."**

My client, Gwyn, was promoted to the CEO of a digital marketing agency. This was an astronomical shift in her responsibilities, how she managed her team, and her time. She was nervous and didn't think she could do it.

We uncovered that her Mother Paradox thrives on taking responsibility for everything so she doesn't look weak or stupid. She spends time filing away unnecessary documents, emails, and minute details wasting an enormous amount of energy to control her team and her time which left her drained at the end of the day with no energy for herself or her family.

Once her pattern became clear, she laughed at the amount of time she spent circling in her head, trying to micromanage her team, thinking she was doing them a favor. Micromanaging is a great paradox time waster.

We began to move from the drop to the pop by practicing letting go of low-level energy that wasn't serving her and any to-do's that she was holding on to that could trip up higher-level thinking.

Once we cleared the cluttered dropbox of her Paradox, we acknowledged its need to feel loved by taking care of and providing comfort to everyone. Then the atmosphere in the room settled, and she relaxed her shoulders and closed her eyes. When she was connected to her vibrant self I asked, "What do you want to spend more time doing that makes you feel alive?"

She took a few breaths as I held the space for her to explore. She took a few minutes then blinked her eyes open and shared that her vibrant self desired even more quiet time, time to stop talking and to listen to herself and her team. It was important to actively listen to their feedback, desires, and dreams, and to listen and respond with heart. Active listening would allow her to get out of the weeds of the detailed Excel spreadsheet and instead create trusting relationships. Active listening was the key to being the type of CEO she wanted to be.

Finally, I asked her, "What are you here to do?" She replied, "**I am here to** embody a CEO bird's-eye mindset."

"Tell me more about that."

"A bird's-eye view gives me space to be visionary and see what's happening on the ground. It doesn't mean I'm on the ground doing the work, picking up each and every seed that falls to the ground. I'm the eyes in the sky to lead the way."

"And why is that important?"

"It's important because I can't take responsibility for everything."

"And why is that important?"

"Because that would be one-sided and I wouldn't get anything done."

"And why is that important?"

"Because I want to build a team I can trust and that can trust me."

"Why is that important?"

Gwyn shifted in her seat, a smile blooming on her lips. "Because we want to work in a values-based culture with heart."

She reached her Clear Concept statement:

**I am here to** embody a CEO bird's-eye view.

**And this is important because** I want to create a values-based culture with heart.

Knowing why you are here and why it's important embodies you in commitment, making you responsible for providing the outcome, regardless of how it happens. You know how you need to show up each and every day to create what you are most committed to creating, simply by who you are being.

This is the vision; the details come later.

We cannot control the outcome of life. Instead, we control our commitment to why it's important and are willing to do whatever it takes. Writing and declaring your clear concept moves it into existence. This is the power of affirmation work, mantras, and positive self-talk.

The first step of making an idea real is to take the idea out of your head. Using your sense of touch—pen to paper—and your sense of sound—thoughts into words—you alert your subconscious that this statement is what you believe. And not only do you believe it, but you wholeheartedly know it is true.

This is your truth. Speak it into power and breathe life into its every word, every day.

**I am here to** _____.

**And this is important because** _____.

Now that you have your clear concept, you are ready to make it real in real time.

## CLEAR STEP 2: LEGIT AND LONG-LASTING

*Legit and Long-Lasting Declaration: "I will…and the first step is to…"*

The first concert I ever went to was MC Hammer on Halloween night in the early '90s, and I'm going to guess that you've heard the song "2 Legit 2 Quit," but I highly doubt you've seen the music video, which, mind you, is 14 minutes long.

## BUILD YOUR CLEAR VISION

In the video, MC Hammer sets out to knock Michael Jackson off the hip-hop and R&B throne and prove his status as the best hip-hop artist of the '90s. MC Hammer recruits The Godfather of Soul, James Brown, to give him the title "Godson of Soul," and at the end of the video, there is a fake cameo from Michael Jackson nodding his approval.

Is this relevant to your Clear Vision? Yes, absolutely, and here's why: MC Hammer had a Clear Vision: I am here to be the Godson of Soul, and this is important because, well, it's a status move.

For those flashy 14 minutes of the music video, MC Hammer was committed, heart and soul, to making this Clear Vision come to life, and he did! But, in real life, we know how that movie ended.

**Is your clear concept 2 Legit 2 Quit?**

These questions will ensure your concept is genuine, will keep your attention, and will endure over time.

Will you stand up for your clear concept, come hell or high water, to see it come to life? Are you committed to sticking it through the ups and downs, the pops and drops to make your idea real?

Are you feeling called from your head to your toe to create this? Does it need to be in the world, and are you the person to do it? Will you leave the world a better place by spending the mental, emotional, and physical energy manifesting this?

Yes or No?

If Yes, please proceed.

If not, go back, release judgment, and do some more brainstorming or prototyping of your idea in the real world to try it on.

Now we are going to get into the HOW of it all, so let's get down to business. This is where we make it happen.

**Long-lasting**

Is this the right time?

Will you focus your time and attention on your clear concept when the rest of the world isn't? Is it going to light you after six months, when you see no result and are exhausted? When you have no time for it anymore?

Yes or No?

If Yes, continue.

We treat time like a person that wants to negotiate with us—as if we could ask time nicely to give us an additional portion,

## BUILD YOUR CLEAR VISION

or to show up when we call or adjust itself to accommodate our whim.

Funny thing, time doesn't want to do that. It doesn't need us at all, so why do we chase it like a lost lover begging that we'll change if it just gives us one last chance? Instead, we need to expand our energy so we can laser focus. More on that in the E (Expanded Energy) of CLEAR Vision.

Show me your calendar, and I can tell you if you relate to time from a pop or drop mindset.

It's time to reinvent your relationship to time and intentionally prioritize time for your clear concept. We have lots of time to do that in Chapter 7, which is about expanding your energy. See what I just did there? I bought you more time.

Why do people come up with groundbreaking ideas in their garage? Because they're in the garage committed to creating their vision.

How did Billie Eilish and her brother Finneas win twelve awards on her debut album? Because they stayed in their tiny house and recorded it daily, nightly, and without wavering on "is this something we should be spending so much time on?"

Why do Olympians win gold medals? They wake up at 4 am to practice because they are committed to their vision of gold.

## FIND YOUR CLEAR VISION

Future visionaries are in their garages and bedrooms at this very moment creating ideas that are ready to explode, and I want you to be at the forefront of your own reinvention wave.

From this moment forward, ask, "Is now the right time?"

Yes.

Your Paradox will have you wait until you are ready…but that's a funny place to be because "ready" is rarely defined; it's a moving target. "Getting ready" is an avoidance technique. There's always more to do and get ready for.

I can't tell you the number of potential clients that tell me they feel fuzzy and stuck and want to create something new and big in their life but aren't ready, and they want to work with me, but they need to get ready first. There's always something "out there" to do before doing the work. Waiting simply keeps you in the dropbox, waiting for the perfect moment to pop (which, mind you, is right now).

If Gwyn waited until she was "ready" to create her vision for CEO *until* she was CEO, she would have been too late. She would have brought the same micromanaging energy to the new role that she had in her last. And she would have gotten the same results.

We proceeded with her vision. She repeated her clear concept: **"I am here to** embody a CEO bird's-eye mindset, **and this is important because** I want to create a values-based culture with heart."

**BUILD YOUR CLEAR VISION**

I said to her, "Awesome, now we need to create the experience of what it looks like to bring your vision to life." I asked, "What will be present when your Clear Vision is complete?"

Gwyn thought about it for a bit and began by sharing some of the qualities she appreciated in a trusting relationship that includes active listening, connection, and acknowledgment. She also recognized that to become a higher-level leader she was going to need to trust herself in a deeper way, which meant not avoiding tough conversations and instead, getting curious about everyone's experience. Curiosity was going to be vital in creating a trusting culture.

"What's the first step?" I asked.

She acknowledged that she needed to build more inner trust, a pillar of the Inner Platform, and start having tough conversations. She didn't want to drop this idea on her team at their Monday morning staff meeting, so instead, she said that she would have a breakfast meeting with her team to share.

"I'm going to host a breakfast Friday morning to share my intention of who I'm going to be as CEO."

My client declared: **I will create** an experience of open communication, active listening, and acknowledgment **and the first step is** to book a breakfast meeting with the team to share on Friday morning.

## FIND YOUR CLEAR VISION

Now you are ready to complete the next sentence stem for Legit and Long-lasting.

**I will** _____.

**And my first step is to** _____.

Now, let's expand your energy to match your clear concept.

## CLEAR STEP 3: EXPANDED ENERGY

*I know who I am. Starting today, I am being...*

The space between the dropbox and the pop into a Clear Vision is the Messy Middle, where your Inner Platform lives. The Inner Platform gives you space to practice self-awareness, inner trust, and expanded energy to stay elevated and grow into a person who is living and breathing your vision, and, as a result, become a visionary.

The problem is, most people stay in their dropbox, replaying the stories of why not and what-ifs because of restrictive and stuck energy. Through healing, cleansing, and forgiveness work we can elevate beyond the repetitive patterns we've been living and become the person we desire to be.

This is important because in order to laser focus on our Clear Vision we have to expand our energy. Laser focus is like a

## BUILD YOUR CLEAR VISION

pair of scissors. You have to open them really wide to get to the center of your piece of paper, and as you cut towards the middle, the wide arc of the scissor blades tighten, get closer together, and end up cutting a straight line towards the middle of the paper, the intended target. Expand your energy like a pair of scissors and cut quickly towards your vision.

Chapter 7 is all about how to embody expanded energy, so let's get prepped for how to pop from the dropbox so you can open up and be ready to receive the energy.

**In the past, what's stopped you from creating your vision?**

Write it down. Or steal from these universal stopping blocks.

Not knowing how to do it

Not doing it perfectly

Afraid of looking stupid

Afraid of looking like a smarty pants

Afraid of failure

Afraid of success

Afraid of what your father would say

Afraid of what your friends would say

## FIND YOUR CLEAR VISION

Afraid your partner will leave you

Afraid you'll leave your partner

Afraid of wasting time

Afraid of working hard

Afraid you'll lose your job

Afraid of being stuck in your job

Calling yourself out on what's stopping you is a signal to your sympathetic nervous system that these so-called threats are something we see and feel and can look at through a new lens. The Paradox has been protecting us from our true desires for a long time, throwing up blind spots and shadows of stories we've held onto for years.

Now you get to choose outside of the dropbox.

Each and every day you get to choose again, and again, and again. Every moment is a choice moment. Time will continually loop a universal stopping block story until you heal, cleanse, and release the energy it's been holding onto for years or sometimes decades.

When you practice the self-awareness technique of choice, you've immediately raised your consciousness and expanded your energy. Like a pair of scissors, you open the arc of the blades up really wide and shift the blade to the right or left, and you get a totally different shape. Choose to shift the slightest bit in another direction and the outcome will reflect a new path.

Releasing your universal stopping block story opens space for new energy.

You may remember cutting snowflakes from folded paper when you were growing up. I remember the thick paper-bag feel of the recycled off-white construction paper, which I would fold in half, and half again and again until it was a tight square and then begin to cut out little triangles and half-moons, eventually enough to make a small pattern.

Then the magic really happened. You would unfold the paper, one fold at a time, to reveal a unique snowflake pattern. Sometimes it worked out beautifully, sometimes it looked like a hot mess. The point being, it was an experiment, and there was always another piece of paper to start again.

Let's play pretend. Imagine cutting a piece of paper with scissors in any way you want. You get to choose, and cut again and again. The playfulness of a childlike mind loosens up the structure of everyday life. You'll feel an openness in your chest, your shoulders will roll off the unwanted tension, your breath will release and re-enter your body with ease as you focus on the here and now.

## FIND YOUR CLEAR VISION

You are safe in the Messy Middle, playing and creating. There is more paper to practice with—you can't mess it up. It's play. Gift yourself the wiggle room to trust yourself to play.

Look towards your future vision with a playful and open mind, and ask yourself:

**Who do I need to be to live in the Messy Middle a little longer?**

**What energetic qualities do I need to embody?**

Play

Fun

Trust

Curiosity

Patience

Abundance

Love

**Who do I need to be to bring my Clear Vision to life?**

Visionary

## BUILD YOUR CLEAR VISION

Strong

Bold

Divine

Confident

Daring

Effervescent

Gwyn told me it felt risky to trust herself. She double-checked her work and the work of her team. She was over-prepared for meetings and felt haphazard in her day. Time would spiral past her, and she noticed by the end of the day she was left feeling lost and unsteady as if she didn't accomplish everything she wanted to.

We looked at what was risky about trusting herself, and how that made her feel in her body. Immediately she felt a tightness in her chest with an overarching hurry-up clock chasing her from behind.

After some reflection, we turned it around. The double-checking was a symptom of not trusting herself. And, in fact, the fear was keeping her in a loop of her Paradox—doing the same thing that got her to where she was today: being a powerful president, but not being the CEO she wanted to be. So we looked at the opposite of not trusting herself, which is a clue into what was missing in her Inner Platform:

"What would it look like to trust yourself?" I asked.

I could see her shoulders drop and release the energy she was holding. She loosened up as flow and white space entered her body. She said that she would invest in herself and her wellbeing. Again looping back to the bird's-eye CEO mindset, she knew that trust would give her space to be curious and visionary, which landed us on her expanded energy statement:

**"I know who I am. Starting today, I am being** curious, visionary, and trusting myself."

If you have a sense of what feeling or energetic quality is missing for you, ask yourself what it would look like to be that way. If you want to feel curious, what would it look like to be curious? This will give you a laser-focused insight into who you need to be starting today to create your Clear Vision.

**Starting today, I am being** _____.

Now we know what we are creating and declare that it is needed in the world right now. We have the energetic qualities of who we need to be to create it, and now it's time to decide what success looks like.

**BUILD YOUR CLEAR VISION**

## CLEAR STEP 4: ASPIRATIONAL SUCCESS

*I know what success looks like.*

The letter A borrows from the SMART model of goal setting, with a twist. Traditionally the A in the SMART model is for Achievable. If you knew how to create and achieve your Clear Vision, you would have already done it.

You don't need this book to reinvent something you could invent from the get-go. I'm not here to lead you down a path of achievable goal setting. Achievable creates change, yes, but does it transform? Rarely.

Achievable has been there, done that. Achievable will create change, a shift in what's different from today to tomorrow, but we're in the business of making ideas real—of dreaming so big with heart, soul, and compassion that even your presence is going to light people aflame with inspiration. We need aspirational success to light that fire—the aspirational vision that pulls you out of bed and forward with ambition and purpose.

Defining your goals, dreams, and intentions will keep you moving purposefully toward your Clear Vision. Aspirational success is the metrics, milestones, and intended results needed to achieve your Clear Vision at a high level of success.

**FIND YOUR CLEAR VISION**

## What does aspirational success look like?

Some clients want to play small here, to create a doable goal. Consider someone who sets a goal to get promoted in their job.

I would ask, "Why is that important?"

"To get a raise."

"Why is that important?"

"To feed my family."

"Why is that important?"

"So we don't go broke."

Okay, you're boring me here. Feeding your family, making more money, I get it, that's all within the realm of achievable.

What does it look like to be donating 20 percent of your income to nonprofits that you wholeheartedly love and start volunteering at your local community theater?

What does aspirational success look like while you are bringing in money not only for your family, but you've retired your parents, have a beach house, and your non-profit foundation is thriving?

## BUILD YOUR CLEAR VISION

What does aspirational success look like when you are so aligned with your whole self that you've written a book a year for the last five years and your latest just hit the *New York Times* bestseller list?

What does that look like?

Better yet, what does it feel like? Paint me a picture of you living wholeheartedly, basking in the aspirational success of your life. This is your dream made real. Get your favorite tasty beverage, turn on some relaxing instrumental French pop music, and gift yourself time to journal on these questions for at least thirty minutes, maybe more. And if you don't have time to drop the book and do it now, then schedule time. Your success is non-negotiable.

**What is going to bring you immersive amounts of joy?** Write it down!

**What have you launched?**

**What have you learned?**

**What's no longer the same?**

After your brainstorm, go through the same steps of "should-ing" you did in the clear concept step. Cross out all of the things you know you can achieve without transforming. You are an ambitious, highly-driven person. I bet you can get a promotion with your eyes closed.

What would it look like to be in the C-suite, start your own business, or move to a foreign country without speaking the language? What would it look like to be fully present in your marriage? How would it feel to be that person?

**Success looks like** _____.

## Massive, Macro, and Mini Milestones

Now we are going to get into the "how" of your vision. I've purposefully set aside the logical, rational left brain, but now it's time to pick it back up and work in unison with our right brain. Most creative people have access to both sides of their brain, and each works with the other in tandem. It's a myth that creative people are only right-brained. They need their logical left brain to make ideas real, and here's how we are going to do it in your life.

There are three types of milestones in your Clear Vision journey: massive, macro, and mini. Most people have big dreams but never take the first step. Here's how to get into action with a fool-proof system for creating aspirational success.

### *Massive Mindset Shifts*

Massive mindset shifts are what you need to bring your Clear Vision to life, which you created in Step 3: Expanded Energy.

We've all experienced change—a change in the weather, a change in a habit, or a change in job—but what does it mean to transform?

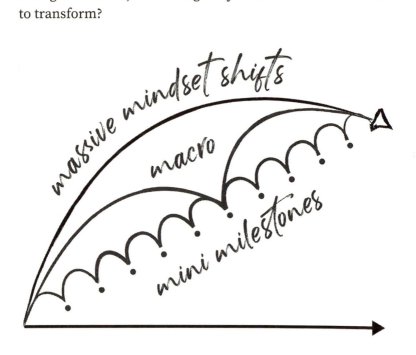

A transformation takes place when what *was* no longer *is*. It's a commitment to a new way of being with no turning back. It's when a caterpillar becomes a butterfly. Caterpillars don't spend half of their precious life in the cocoon only to come out on the other side as another version of a caterpillar. No, they come out transformed, and this is what we are aiming for.

Transformation can happen in an instant, if you choose to believe in it right here, right now, and for always. Or a transformation can be birthed, over time. It's a choice you make every day that reflects your commitment to your reinvention.

Let's pause for a morbid moment. Donald Miller—storyteller, author, and entrepreneur—shared this idea in his recent book. Imagine, one year from today, 365 days from this moment, you die. I know, I'm sorry for your loss. At your funeral celebration, a dear friend is reading your eulogy of all the things that you've accomplished in life.

What have you overcome in the past 365 days? And when you overcame that thing, what did it give you? Who are you as a result of overcoming that moment?

That person, 365 days from today, who has overcome your biggest obstacle? That is you, transformed. When you are transformed, who have you become?

Take sovereignty over who you are becoming, and be them right now.

This is a reinvention to massively transform your life, livelihood, and leadership as a result of who you are being.

**Massive Mindset Shift: Who do you want to be when your vision is complete?**

Be joy-filled, brave, and balanced.

## BUILD YOUR CLEAR VISION

Be daring, sparkling, and decisive.

If you want to get super tactile, consider how you want to influence your career, business, or industry. Write three mindsets, or adjectives, that will catapult you into who you need to be to create your Clear Vision.

**Massive Mindset Shift:**

1.

2.

3.

## Macro Milestones

Macro milestones are the overarching umbrella that holds together the beginning, middle, and end of your Clear Vision. It's what you are going to create to complete your vision.

We don't need to know all of the details. That would keep us drowning in the weeds of "what did I get myself into?" Instead, we are simply picking the top three milestones, and you can consider that today is a milestone. Therefore, you started your Clear Vision today. Congratulations!

**First Step:** To start today, done! Add it to your calendar today and cross it off. Marking it complete is a signal to your subconscious that you accomplished something and are moving forward.

**Middle Step:** What's the halfway point? It may be easier to look at the third and final milestone before filling in this one so you can see the ending, then you'll know the halfway point.

**Final Vision:** Okay, yes, there will be multiple steps between today and your complete Clear Vision, but we are creating the umbrella bird's-eye view before diving into the weeds on purpose. Your Paradox loves to roll around and get lost in the weeds of tasks, to-do lists, and gold stars. Macro milestones keep you elevated and intentional with a place to go.

Let's get creative.

**What is the final intention for your vision?**

**What's present?**

**What did you put into the world?**

If you are a visual person, you could create a tangible vision board like we used to do in grade school.

In my studio, I have images that are worn on the edges, taped onto the wall from Pottery Barn and West Elm summer catalogs scenes. You know, the ones with perfectly positioned margaritas on an outdoor patio set next to a lake or overly-styled beach house in Malibu? That's where I'm living when my future vision is complete.

Write it down. Sketch it out, cut it up, vision board it. Create it as if it's already a reality. You are bringing it to life with your thoughts, feelings, and actions. A Clear Vision of your third and final massive milestone will alert your subconscious that "Okay, cool, this is what we are doing. How can I help?"

**Macro Milestones**

First Step:

Middle Step:

Final Vision:

*Mini Milestones*

**What's the first baby step?** You've completed the biggest hurdle: you are starting. What's the first step you can take after you set this book down today? Make it a small one. It doesn't have to be a big deal.

We are training our minds to hold expanded energy and small tactical, laser-focused energy. We are in the business of intentional and consistent action, to make the long-lasting vision a reality.

## FIND YOUR CLEAR VISION

- Call Susan and tell her about my vision.

- Set a reminder on my phone to tell my future self who I am becoming.

- Buy some delicious Earl Grey tea to drink as I create my vision board.

- Book time in my calendar to begin.

**Mini Milestone**

**Write down your first baby step, and by when it will be complete.**

- Call Susan and tell her about my vision **at noon.**

- Set a reminder on my phone to tell my future self who I am becoming **for 2:22 pm every day this month.**

- Buy some delicious Earl Grey tea to drink as I create my vision board **this afternoon before dinner.**

- Book time in my calendar to begin **right now.**

## Book It

Your future self can't be trusted. I've said this to clients, and they are offended. "You don't know me! When I say I'm going to do something, I do it."

## BUILD YOUR CLEAR VISION

Not true. When it comes to your calendar, your future self cannot be trusted. You'll feel tired, or not ready, and you'll find anything else to do. There is that juicy email you didn't respond to! Ding, an email just came in—let's see who needs something! You'll be seduced by your Paradox to create anything other than your Clear Vision that you just manifested.

Connect to your most vibrant self and ask, **"If I'm being honest, how much time do I need to block out in my calendar each day to get to the middle step?"**

And then book it; it's non-negotiable.

Adding time to your calendar will do two things: first, it will alert your conscious and subconscious mind that your vision is a priority. And secondly, it will disable your future self from discounting your choices. Booking time will prevent your Paradox from sneaking in at the last minute to tell you that it would be so much more fun to go out with friends for drinks rather than stick to your dry January. Or to hit snooze and skip your morning ritual. Now is the time—book it.

After expanding her energy, Gwyn realized she was not taking full ownership of the CEO role in her mind; it was something that was "out there" versus who she was being on the inside. Who she wanted to be as CEO was a thought, but she hadn't let the thought move into a feeling. She wasn't coming from a place of full commitment to embodying her CEO role. Her Aspirational Success statement became:

"**Success looks like** radically trusting myself and my heart with my team and clients. And the first baby step is to book a time to meditate."

Notice this lands very differently than it would if she was taking responsibility for her team and clients, but that's not the intention. She's trusting herself and her heart first and bringing that energy to her team. Massive milestones always come first. Macro and mini milestones will not work unless you are fully committed to who you are becoming.

**Success looks like** _____.

Now, let's get to the really fun part.

## CLEAR STEP 5: ROOTED IN CELEBRATION

Does your Clear Vision push you out of your comfort zone?

Yes or No?

Does your Clear Vision light you up?

Yes or No?

If No, go back to Step 1: Clear Concept, and start over.

No one celebrates with more pure, unfiltered joy than a toddler. Ever notice how a two-year-old can go from an utter

## BUILD YOUR CLEAR VISION

meltdown to complete contentment in moments? First, they're on the floor of the grocery store aisle, grabbing anything on the bottom shelf and flinging it away because they weren't allowed a lollipop at checkout. Then, moments later, after you have dragged them from the grocery store under one arm while carrying groceries with the other, and strapped them into their car seat, dodging the sideways glances and knowing smiles of other shoppers, the little angel is clapping their chubby hands together, and blowing raspberry bubbles to a song on the radio with a good bassline.

A child's emotional rollercoaster may not be the best example, but notice how they are willing to pop and drop at a moment's notice? Their emotional range is what we want to embrace: the ability to wildly celebrate life, even when it's messy.

Creativity is fun. It's playful and filled with pure imagination. Energy is contagious, reproduces quickly, and can be created on-demand through intentional celebration. I believe in celebration. It's one of my core values, and it's who I aspire to be. I celebrate small wins like a two-year-old who just won the Super Bowl. Signed a new client? *WIN!* Made it in and out of Costco in forty-five minutes? *WIN!*

Here are examples of how my clients have celebrated big and small wins:

Celebrate by going on a shopping spree in Melbourne.

Celebrate by taking private dance lessons.

## FIND YOUR CLEAR VISION

Celebrate by buying flowers.

Celebrate by getting a manicure every Friday.

Celebrate by taking my son out for ice cream.

Celebrate by going to the movies by myself on a Tuesday.

Celebrate by sleeping in on Sunday.

Celebrate by making truffles this weekend.

Celebrate by booking a trip to South Africa this summer.

This is your life, your wellbeing, and your celebration. Make it count. You deserve it.

Celebration signals your brain to release dopamine, a "feel-good" neurotransmitter, which creates joy and happiness. Celebration is nourishment for the brain. It's important to celebrate your milestones because it creates fuel to continue with a high level of energy. Expanding your spectrum of feelings from meh to joy, compassion, excitement, and even utter delight is yours to own.

Gwyn's final Clear Vision declaration turned out to be just what she needed to create the experience she desired for herself, her new role, and her team.

**I am here to** embody a CEO bird's-eye mindset.

## BUILD YOUR CLEAR VISION

**And this is important because** I want to create a values-based culture with heart.

**I will** create an experience of open communication, active listening, and acknowledgment.

**And the first step is to** book a breakfast meeting with the team to share.

**Starting today, I am being** curious, visionary, and trusting myself.

**Success looks like** radically trusting myself and my heart with my team and clients.

**I will celebrate by** taking the team out for drinks every other month and booking myself a massage every month.

Your Clear Vision has been defined, you have the roadmap, and you have the GPS to the life you most desire. Now go have fun and come back to begin the next chapter when your cheeks hurt from smiling and your feet are tired from dancing.

Hold on to the pop of your Clear Vision because it's where you are going to operate from day in and day out. Your Clear Vision has been birthed, manifested, and truer words have never been spoken. Step into that power. It's your power. Allow it to bubble over and wash over you. Allow the blood-pumping energy of having defined your purpose to resonate deep within your bones. It is safe to feel this powerful; it is safe to own all of you as someone who can create your vision and make it real.

I expect nothing less of you.

It is your radical responsibility to shine from who you are meant to be with every macro and mini choice, to choose outside of the dropbox of the Paradox, and to celebrate who you are becoming, starting today.

**How will you celebrate when your Clear Vision is complete?**

**How will you celebrate today?**

---

**BRIGHT TOOL:**
**CLEAR VISION FRAMEWORK**

Download the Clear Vision Framework at
www.bebrightlisa.com/findyourclearvision-book

---

## STEP 1: CLEAR CONCEPT

What do people ask me for advice on?

What conversations do I want to be a part of in the future?

## BUILD YOUR CLEAR VISION

What do I want to spend more time doing that makes me feel alive?

What do most people think is true, but I know there's another way to think about it?

When I'm living my life from my Clear Vision, what does my day look like?

### Ikigai Questions

**What do you love?** (Your passion)

**What are you good at?** (Your profession)

**What does the world need?** (Your mission)

**What can you get paid for?** (Your occupation)

If there were no limits, what would you do?

What are you here to do?

Why is this important?

**I am here to** _____.

**And this is important because** _____.

## STEP 2: LEGIT AND LONG-LASTING

Is your clear concept 2 Legit 2 Quit? (Y/N)

Is this the right time? (Y/N)

What will be present when my Clear Vision is complete?

What's the first step?

**I will** _____.

**And the first step is to** _____.

## STEP 3: EXPANDED ENERGY

Who do I need to be to live in the Messy Middle longer?

What energetic qualities do I need to embody?

Who do I need to be to bring my Clear Vision to life?

**Starting today I am being** _____.

## STEP 4: ASPIRATIONAL SUCCESS

What does aspirational success look like?

## BUILD YOUR CLEAR VISION

What is going to bring me immersive amounts of joy?

What have I launched?

What have I learned?

What's no longer the same?

**Massive Mindset Shift:**

Who do I want to be when my vision is complete?

1.

2.

3.

**Macro Milestones:**

What is the final intention for my vision?

What's been created?

What's launched?

What's transformed?

What did I put into the world?

1. Today

2.

3. Clear Vision Realized

How much time do I need to block out in my calendar each day to get to the middle step?

**Mini Milestones:**

What's the first baby step?

When will I do it?

**Success looks like** _____.

## STEP 5: ROOTED IN CELEBRATION

How will I celebrate when my Clear Vision is complete?

How will I celebrate today?

**I will celebrate by** _____.

Now that you've got your CLEAR Vision declaration (and you're celebrating!), let's focus on your energy.

Chapter 7

# CREATE AND EXPAND YOUR ENERGY

THERE ARE TWO TYPES OF PEOPLE: THOSE WHO CREATE energy and those who drain it.

Just like water down the drain, your best ideas, biggest insights, and award-winning concepts may have floated away because you are not budgeting your energy. And the sad thing is you turned the faucet off. Spending energy worrying about trivial things and trying to accommodate your Paradox is an excellent way to muddy the waters.

When I started my coaching practice in 2016, I didn't charge for an introductory session. Instead, I would invite potential clients to an hour-long session for free to see if we were a match for coaching. This one particular week I had two introductory sessions scheduled with male executives, one in Silicon Valley, and the other in Oklahoma.

## CREATE AND EXPAND YOUR ENERGY

Both individuals canceled an hour before our scheduled time. Via text.

That afternoon I had a call with my coach and told her the story of how I was wronged. I dove into my dropbox of Poor Me, moaning and groaning about how "They don't value me! They don't value my time. Am I just a vendor they can cancel on? I saved time for them, and this is the respect I get? Screw those guys!!"

She stopped me. "Lisa, where do you feel this energy in your body?"

And I said, "I feel like a vice is tightening around my chest, and it's hard to breathe. I feel a bubbling roar of energy in my heart that I want to rip out and stomp on."

Have you ever been set off because you thought someone side-eyed you? Or a word someone casually tossed into a conversation pushed you over the top and you ruminate on it for days? Or maybe a lover didn't kiss you in front of their co-workers? "What's up with that? Are they embarrassed by me? Am I not good enough for them?"

I needed a powerful release to shake off the energy that was bouncing back and forth inside my chest. I put Rage Against the Machine's song "Killing in the Name" in my AirPods, turned it up till my eardrums bled, dropped to the floor, and did mountain climbers until I could barely breathe and the song was done.

## FIND YOUR CLEAR VISION

I raged against the thoughts and energy I had created in my body. I released and renewed my energy in a four-minute song.

The two men canceling on me left me feeling unseen, undervalued, and unloved. It triggered a deeper wound in me, stemming from a childhood experience when I felt the same way. I could have stayed there, wallowing in the anger and resentment, but instead, I recognized it was a choice moment. I knew, on the other side of my Rage Against the Machine moment, was me and my Clear Vision. I knew if I discharged the negative thoughts that I was undervalued and unseen, I could recharge with my self-created positive energy, and once again feel safe in who I am.

After the song was over I popped up, smiling to myself with a renewed sense of strength. I had released the negative energy safely and productively and could refocus on my day ahead. Don't get me wrong, in my early 20s, I would have thrown back two double Bourbons, gone out clubbing until 3 am on a weekday night, then back to work at the design studio in the morning.

The Paradox Pattern is a tricky little scientist who embeds energy and experiences from the past into your cellular memory, often using alcohol, drugs, sex, or other addictions to either downplay or enlarge negative feelings, which becomes part of your story, and, over time, your personal identity. Sticking around like a memory, repeating a thought pattern that manifests itself in your choices, behaviors, and emotions.

## CREATE AND EXPAND YOUR ENERGY

When your body feels your thoughts, like fear or sadness, for example, it releases energy to support the thought "I am scared," which starts a hamster wheel of the cellular energy of your past, which informs your future of how you should feel. Your heart beats faster. Your breath becomes rapid and shallow. Your blood pressure starts to rise and your cheeks flush. Your brain signals to your pupils to dilate so you can have better tunnel vision to focus on the threatening thought—*I'm scared*.

At this point, your muscles become tense, you may even begin shaking. Some people get goosebumps. Tears start to well up in your eyes and your saliva decreases, as your mouth goes dry. Your thoughts continue to go downhill as you think, "I couldn't even speak up if I wanted to. I need water!" Your blood sugar level increases to support the energy needed to protect yourself. Your immune system shuts down, and your brain has trouble focusing on small tasks because it feels it needs to focus 100 percent on this potential threat.

That energetic reaction takes fifteen to thirty seconds. Crazy, right? Now, instead of moving towards your Clear Vision, you are busy trying to make your past self feel whole again, for the next hour, or days, depending on how long you hold on to the energy.

I honor the energetic journey you have been on in this life. Studies show that we carry residual, ancestral trauma inside of our body, and without the tools and expertise to release the trauma, it stays buried, hibernating until called upon when we are triggered.

## FIND YOUR CLEAR VISION

Dr. Valerie Rein, author of *Patriarchy Stress Disorder*, says that trauma is "any experience that makes you feel unsafe in your fullest authentic expression and leads to developing trauma adaptations to keep you safe."

Trauma can be a life-altering experience, one that includes violence, rape, segregation, misogyny, and patriarchy. Trauma is often simmering under the surface of your life experience, being fed by the media, social media, religion, or sometimes your partner or family.

Corporate America has struggled with seeing and hearing people of color and women's experiences as valid and true—which, because of the Paradox Pattern, women have fallen victim to, downplaying their stories in an attempt to be relatable and not poke the bear. I've had multiple clients who have been given substantial severance packages to keep "what happened at work" quiet.

Your past is your truth. I acknowledge all the experiences you have had, how you were raised, where you grew up, the color of your skin, how you identify as an individual human. Your unique life experience has crafted and created the person you are today, and who you are becoming.

But, when you are spending your time spinning stories to be relatable or fit in, rather than being you, you are wasting your creative energy—the energy that is right behind the Paradox, waiting for you to choose again, outside the default story of being quiet, fitting in, shame, blame, and no gain.

## CREATE AND EXPAND YOUR ENERGY

Diminishing your power by spinning stories is distracting you from your Clear Vision.

I know this is true because I was distracted for years when I first had my children and owned my business. I functioned with a racing, scattered energetic level of survival energy and thought it was normal. Years later my body gave me the clear signal that it wasn't down for this type of energy anymore, but I didn't listen until it popped up as shingles on my face and in my eye. Many breakdowns and breakouts later, I learned how to discharge and recharge my energy on purpose.

Let's shift our energy now, together.

Did you ever get butterflies when your high school crush said "hi" to you, and love stole your breath? Or goosebumps when you thought of going to see your favorite band in concert or a DJ at the club? Or a tingling sensation when you did something naughty and didn't get caught?

You've been generating your energy for years—now let's do it with purpose.

The type of personal energy I'm talking about is:

When you jump up and down because you are so excited, and the energy needs to escape.

When you lean into an idea, and you can see the outcome as if it were already happening.

## FIND YOUR CLEAR VISION

When you trust your intuition so clearly you know when you are a "Hell Yes" or a "Hell No" for something.

When you have ideas seemingly pop up out of nowhere and you act on them with conviction.

When you know exactly what to say.

This is because you are emotionally wealthy.

You are an idea magnet.

You are open and receptive to divine downloads.

You are your fully embodied vibrant self.

You surround yourself with people who have the same energetic frequency.

You have emotional boundaries to structure your wellbeing.

And you manage the flow of new energy with ease.

Learning how to discharge and recharge your energy is fundamental to building your Inner Platform to release the negative energy that is gluing together unwelcome patterns. The question is: how?

Expanding your personal energy is essential to building your Inner Platform and personal brand. Sharing who you are is innately an energetic exchange and is fundamental to being in a relationship. Personal branding is, after all, personal. Business branding is a one-way conversation of a made-up ideal identity that the target audience is meant to connect with and buy from. Personal branding is an energetic exchange—your mindset connecting to someone else's.

Learning how to expand and budget your energy will create a sense of safety and confidence to be with more experiences, people, and opportunities. Energy is ever-flowing, and always available. With the power of choosing your energy source and being in the practice of charging, discharging, and recharging energy you become an energetic icon.

Trauma is energy. And so is full authentic expression. The tools in this chapter will help you feel safe in your power—because you are a powerful thriving being worthy of ever-flowing energy. It is safe to play with creative energy, safe to step outside of the patterns of thoughts and feelings in the mind, and to redefine what it means to be you—radiant, strong, focused, clear, divine, and empowered. You are safe to be seen in your fullest authentic expression. You simply need to practice being this way. Practice staying in the Messy Middle longer.

Jamie Lee Curtis spoke to this when she said, "I believe I can do my job and have a private life. I believe in the separation of church and state. I believe that I don't owe anybody anything once I've done my work. I am by nature a super friendly person, but I also have a very clear boundary of what's appropriate and inappropriate for me to share."

**FIND YOUR CLEAR VISION**

When Jamie Lee Curtis was asked how to stay relevant as a sixty-year-old woman in Hollywood with a career that expands four decades, she told *Fast Company*, "I'm a marketing and advertising exec's dream girl. I have created a personal brand with some integrity."

Clear boundaries have created energetic boundaries for her to do her work and have a private life, and you can do this too.

## CREATIVE PLANNING FOR EXPANDED ENERGY

Your relationship to your mind, body, and soul in the past is a reflection of who you were, not who you are becoming. Gift yourself time and space to have a new relationship by choosing to pop in every moment of your energetic reinvention. Let's try a variety of energetic practices for spiritual energy within you, foundational energy to support you, and connection energy with others.

When I work with clients, we create a roadmap towards their Clear Vision, but only schedule milestones one to three months out. A mini milestone is the perfect middle ground for multi-passionate creative types who are often led astray by shiny object syndrome and find it hard to focus on creating one thing for too long. A smaller chunk of time signals to your mind that this isn't forever; it's just for now, and we can handle a new habit or ritual for the next thirty to ninety days.

## CREATE AND EXPAND YOUR ENERGY

How do you want to experience and embody your energy in thirty days? Do you need to discharge or recharge your energy?

What ideas or experiences do you need to add to elevate your energy?

What do you need to tell yourself when you drop?

What's the first step?

A thirty-day plan will give you wiggle room to pivot, adjust, and redefine what moving forward means to you. It will also create tangible habits you can use as data for the next thirty days.

Remember, the world was not built in a day. It is growing, ebbing, and flowing even as you read this book. Keep your eyes on the prize towards your massive mindset milestones, and remember, it's the mini-steps that will get you there.

To expand energy, we have to create it. Let's play with our energy.

Like a pair of scissors, creative energy is a wide arc of flowing energy, and when you laser focus on a singular goal or intention, your mind will absorb the energy and move toward the target with the precision of a sharp cut.

*Expanded Energy + Laser Focus = Creative Flow*

**FIND YOUR CLEAR VISION**

While in creative flow you lose track of time and space, and creativity bubbles over, popping all around you. Ideas can't be stopped, you can't write fast enough, and your fingers can't keep up. It's as if the world has become your muse. You could dance all day and night, give a speech to a sold-out audience, knock the socks off a client, *and* have the energy to work out afterward.

To pop our energy, we have to focus on the space in between the space. I know, I know—please follow along here. Energy lives in the spaces in between. In between the lightning and thunder, in between the thought "He's the cutest boy I've ever seen!" and the feeling of butterflies.

The space in between lives in our energy centers. The light frequency in between your cells is the glue that makes you whole. Let's treasure, nurture, and nourish the light within our energy centers to expand our energy and creativity.

If you only take one thing from your entire reinvention experience, take this: the heart of self-awareness is to witness your thoughts before they become feelings and turn into actions. Self-awareness gives you the sovereignty to create your life, rather than it creating you, and you can begin by witnessing and playing with your energy centers.

Dynamic, expandable, and replenishable energy lives in between every cell in your body—as tiny beams of light, little pops of energy in your chakras.

**CREATE AND EXPAND YOUR ENERGY**

## CHAKRA ENERGY

Chakras are eight energy centers in your body. Chakra means "wheel" in ancient Hindu texts. Chakras are spiritual energy centers up and down the center of your body and are used in ancient meditation practices. Remember when you felt butterflies? The energy in your Sacral chakra was popping. Your thoughts channel energy through the first chakra, all the way up into the brain and beyond.

Notice where you feel energy in your body right now; it's sending you a signal. Does your throat tighten up when you want to say something controversial? Did your heart burst with love when your kid ran into your arms after a hard day at school? Does your head feel lighter after you meditate? Find which chakra energy centers resonate with you so you can build your self-awareness practice to charge, discharge, and recharge energy to create flow.

### Root, Sacral, and Solar Plexus

The first three chakras—the root, sacral, and solar plexus—are based on our survival animal nature. They are meant to keep us safe, reproducing, and alert. Sure, this was all fine and good when we needed our mind to alert us to a pack of wolves around the corner, and a woman's body was used as a baby-making machine, but we can use it for so many other purposes now.

**FIND YOUR CLEAR VISION**

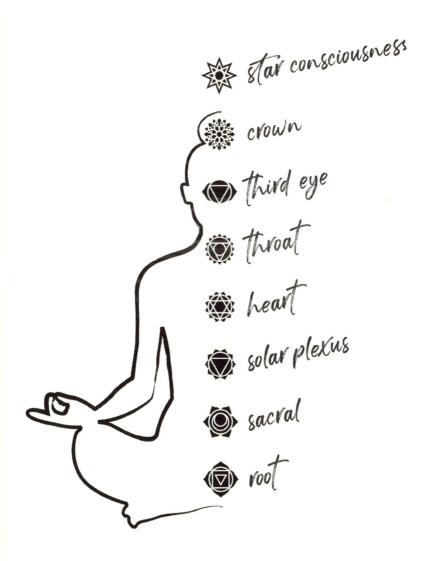

# CREATE AND EXPAND YOUR ENERGY

## *Root Chakra*

The first chakra, located in your pelvic floor at the base of your spine, is the root chakra. Rest the palm of your hand there now to connect to its power. Your root chakra governs your survival energy, sexual feelings, and sexual identity. Think about how much creative energy is spent making love, and in the birthing process. The female body creates a human being inside their body for forty weeks. Unbelievable, right?

Your root chakra is the foundation of your energy centers. It stores and creates an energy of safety and inner trust. The fear of the unknown fights your feelings of safety, so you overcompensate by hurrying to get things done so you have a nice and tidy outcome, trying to control the unknown. Notice when you feel pressure to hurry up to avoid any pain, to get it done, and move forward already.

Ask yourself, "Am I in a hurry to release the pressure of not knowing? Am I in a hurry not to feel discomfort?"

Trauma with a capital T lives here related to sexual abuse, anxiety, and confusion. If you have experienced sexual abuse, I recommend that you work with a trained professional to heal and release energy stored in your root chakra before moving on; otherwise, you may continue to operate on top of stored cellular energy.

**Root Chakra color**: Ruby red

**Discharge energy**: Take deep exhales.

**Recharge energy**: Get into the yoga pose of Warrior One.

**Mantras**: "I am at peace, poised, and safe knowing that all is well."

"I trust myself."

*Sacral Chakra*

The sacral chakra is the birthing place of new ideas, creativity, and creation. It is also the source of sexual desire. Have you ever been in love with someone even though you know they aren't good for you? Or vice versa, you are in a relationship with someone because they look good on paper, but you just don't feel sexy when you are with them? Sexual desire rises from your sacral chakra giving you butterflies—making illogical decisions for you in the name of love.

Social structure, community, family, and cultural stories live here—which, if you are carrying the energy of your ancestors, is why shame, blame, guilt, and a sense of unworthiness may live here too. When the sacral chakra is balanced, you feel safe in relationships and the world; when triggered, you may feel unworthy of love or a victim of your social circumstance.

Emotions reside in the hips, especially when you sit down or drive for much of your day. Moving into a child's pose to release your hips will start to release and renew energy in your sacral chakra.

Ask yourself, "What stories am I holding as true? What would it feel like to release them?"

**Sacral Chakra color**: Bright orange

**Discharge energy**: Do child's pose.

**Recharge energy**: Get into water, dance in the rain, take a shower or a bath.

**Sacral Chakra mantra**: "I release the stories of the past and am worthy of love and respect."

"I am worthy of love."

## Solar Plexus Chakra

Have you had a gut feeling that you should turn left instead of right? You think, "I don't know what it is, but I feel like we should go this way."

You may know someone who can make decisions quickly, and seemingly without effort. These types of people have deep access to the solar plexus chakra. This area of your body is responsible for digestion and the release of food energy. It is too low in your body to be a rational thought. Instead, it's a gut feeling or a hunch that lives above your belly button and below your ribs.

People who have access to the solar plexus set boundaries for themselves and others because they know what's best for them. "If I am being honest, I want this."

The Solar Plexus is the final energy center in your survival animal nature, the last train to leave the station before moving into the upper energy centers. Associated with drive, ambition, and competition, this center, when negatively charged, tries to protect the Ego from what's unpredictable by controlling the world around it, oftentimes trying to prove that it's right and others are wrong.

Ask yourself: "What am I holding on to because I have to be right? If I let this go, what will be released?"

**Solar Plexus Chakra color**: Yellow

**Discharge energy**: Mountain climb or jump up and down.

**Recharge energy**: Hold your arms out wide in a receiving pose with your hands up and breathe deeply for two minutes.

**Solar Plexus Chakra mantra**: "The world is not black and white. I am part of a thriving and colorful world."

"I can be with it all."

## CREATE AND EXPAND YOUR ENERGY

The first three energy centers are to protect and create energy for you to survive. When energy is stuck, it's typically in these three energy centers, which leads to repetitive patterns, wondering, "Why does this always happen to me?"

Using the quick discharging and recharging methods to get back to your self-awareness, the space in between your thoughts and actions will help bring new thoughts of safety, security, and renewal into your body. As you practice releasing unwanted thoughts of self-protection and validation, you'll have more energy to move into a selfless space of love, flow, and gratitude.

### Upper-Level Energy

#### Heart Chakra

The fourth chakra sits in the center of your chest. It is your love center, your internal "G-spot." This energy center is referred to as the "fountain of youth" because it's responsible for repair and rejuvenation, where 1,400 chemicals associated with immunity and growth live.

Your beating heart gives your body rhythm, structure, and flow. It influences your ability to give and receive love for yourself and others. It's your GPS to follow your heart instead of your head.

**FIND YOUR CLEAR VISION**

Your heart is constantly giving you signals when it's in or out of alignment. Think about a time when your partner said something that made your blood boil, or when they said something so sweet you felt your heart burst with love. Blood pressure, rising or falling, and the beating of your heart is a constant reminder of the energy of love generated in your heart chakra.

Ask yourself, "Where can I love myself more?"

**Heart Chakra color**: Green

**Discharge energy**: Shake it off.

**Recharge energy**: Use hand-to-heart breathing.

**Heart Chakra mantra:** "I am worthy of love because I radiate love."

"I am love."

## Throat Chakra

The fifth chakra is at the base of your throat, the tiny nook that rests between your neck and your chest. This is your energy center of creative expression through words, using the vibrations in your voice to share your message and speak your truth. This is where expression and communication live.

## CREATE AND EXPAND YOUR ENERGY

The throat chakra is where I do the majority of my energy work. Before I started doing energy work, without fail, two days before a big presentation or masterclass, my throat would become scratchy. Multiple times I've found myself at the Walgreens pharmacy the day before the presentation with bronchitis or strep throat. I used to self-medicate with a slew of antibiotics to increase my energy, but now that I've recognized the pattern: big presentation = nervous energy = "What if they don't like what I have to say?" = throat closes up.

Have you ever noticed before saying a bold thing, or asking for a promotion, you get a frog in your throat, or you lose your voice? That's your throat chakra giving you a clear signal.

Ask yourself, "What do I need to say to communicate clearly?"

**Throat Chakra color**: Turquoise

**Discharge energy**: Drink water-based liquids.

**Recharge energy**: Visualize the end of a successful conversation or presentation.

**Throat Chakra mantra**: "I am safe speaking my truth because people want to know what I have to say."

"I am the expert."

**FIND YOUR CLEAR VISION**

## *Third Eye Chakra*

The sixth chakra is your third eye, which doesn't sit right in between your eyes; it's an energy center that lives behind your eyes, a few inches back, inside your brain. When aligned with positive flowing energy, it connects you to a higher dimension by releasing hormones like serotonin and melatonin, producing a sleep-wake state common in deep meditation.

When I'm listening to beta and theta wave meditations, which are different sound waves that are meant to connect you to your energy, I focus on my third eye chakra, spinning the rich indigo energy around, exploring the deep crevices, entering a lucid dream-like space between my inner and outer worlds. Call it whatever you like—Universe, Spirit, God, Source energy—connecting to your third eye energy, the space in between our 3D physical world and a 5D spiritual world, feels gorgeous. This is that meditative high that so many people talk about.

Playing with third eye energy will give you radical signs and signals of your future. Flow, ideas, and sparks of ah-ha live there. When the five energy centers below the third eye chakra are aligned and you are willing to sit in the unknown space between this world and the Universe, ideas are born. Creativity, flow, and miracles are released.

When your third eye is not in flow, and energy is trapped, it is hard to see your future, and you feel stuck. The third eye energy is the gateway to your Clear Vision. Without access to seeing your future clearly, it makes it difficult to move forward with inner knowing and self-trust.

If you can't assess this energy, ask yourself: "What energy am I not willing to be with?" Or, "If I could see clearly, what's available to me?"

**Third Eye Chakra color**: Indigo

**Discharge energy**: Use any of the previous energy center practices to dislodge stuck energy to clear a pathway to your third eye.

**Recharge energy**: Sit in meditation with beta and theta instrumental music for 15+ minutes.

**Third Chakra mantra**: "I'm open and receptive to creativity."

"I'm available for miracles."

## Crown Chakra

The seventh chakra is your crown chakra which sits above the top of the head, floating a little bit outside of your body but inside your energetic aura. Your crown chakra is the realm of awareness and consciousness, your portal to higher consciousness.

**FIND YOUR CLEAR VISION**

When your crown chakra's energy is harmonious, you are connected to unlimited inspiration and inner trust. Time is irrelevant when you are in flow with inspiration. This is your queendom where you are fully in creative expression, aligned with your vision and purpose, stepping into your full power.

But, the reverse, when you are not energetically connected to your crown, is where anxiety and pressure may live, egging you on to believe you are not enough. Maybe you are trying to please others by going down their path, or trying too hard to prove yourself as capable, which limits your time and energy.

If you can't access your crown chakra energy, ask yourself: "Am I on my path, or following someone else's? Where and what am I being led by?"

**Crown Chakra color**: Pure white

**Discharge energy**: Sage the air around you or remove unwanted energy by rhythmically waving energy away around your head and shoulders.

**Recharge energy**: Sit in meditation and imagine a thousand-petal lotus at the crown of your head, pulling healing and nourishing light through it into your crown and body.

**Crown Chakra mantra**: "I am powerful beyond measure."

"I am abundant."

**CREATE AND EXPAND YOUR ENERGY**

## *Star Consciousness Chakra*

The eighth chakra is your star consciousness, located twelve to sixteen inches above your head, and is often not included when talking about the seven major chakras, but this is foundational to connecting to and expressing your Clear Vision because this energy center is your connection to the universe, to all that is. When connected to your star consciousness energy, you are ready to receive creative downloads, universal truths, and divine connection. Because your star consciousness is not connected to your body in the physical sense or embedded in the nervous system or the cellular patterns you are trying to break from, you can make choices outside of your ancestral thought patterns. Your Paradox feels safe being in the unknown because your star consciousness is activated and guided by the quantum field of energy that surrounds every one of us.

When you are not energetically connected to your star consciousness, you feel ungrounded and unclear, which often manifests itself as cynicism. People judge and don't like what they can't understand.

The difference between your crown and star chakra is that the crown is your relationship to the universe, and the star chakra is humankind's connection to our collective energy. This is what shamans and healers are talking about when they say, "We are one."

Ask yourself, "How can I connect my intention to the world? What does the world need?"

**Star Consciousness Chakra color**: Iridescent white, the presence of all colors in the spectrum

**Discharge energy**: Cross your hands over your heart and hold space for yourself as you do a series of cleansing breaths to reconnect to yourself before reconnecting to universal energy.

**Recharge energy**: Sit in meditation and imagine a bright iridescent light surrounding all of your body, protecting and nourishing you with the power of universal connection and abundance.

**Star Consciousness mantra**: "I am one with the Universe. I am connected to all humankind."

"We are one."

## HOW DO YOU WANT TO FEEL?

Reinvention is about creating the future in advance.

You have a Clear Vision of what you are creating in the future, but what happens when you wake up tomorrow? What do you eat for breakfast, and how do you nourish your body? How do you want to experience energy in your body?

In *The Power of Full Engagement* by Tony Schwartz and Jim Loehr, they write, "Performance, health, and happiness are grounded in the skillful management of energy. The number

## CREATE AND EXPAND YOUR ENERGY

of hours in a day is fixed, but the quantity and quality of energy available to us are not. It is our most precious resource. The more we take responsibility for the energy we bring to the world, the more empowered and productive we become."

I've seen it time and time again. Someone has their Clear Vision mapped out in their calendar, which is filled with steps to create the future they desire, but their master plan goes into a tailspin of "With all of this work, my calendar is booked. I don't have time to work out, much less go to the grocery store!" And just like that, the paradox of "self-care is selfish" has won.

If you are the type of person who in a heartbeat crosses off your plan to go to the gym when something, anything else arises, it's time for a new game plan. What is going to happen if you continue to backlog your nourishment and physical wellbeing? My guess is probably more of the same, more excuses, and exhaustion.

Without the foundational elements to nourish your body, created and booked in advance, your body won't be able to support your vision.

Let's flip the script. How do you want to feel a year from now when your Clear Vision is rocking and rolling? For example, let's say your Clear Vision is to create a global consulting business with fifty ideal clients.

How do you want to feel when that is done?

## FIND YOUR CLEAR VISION

Freedom, agency, fulfillment!

What's your plan to feel that way tomorrow?

Oftentimes, my clients answer that "I can't feel that way until I have a successful consulting practice." Or, "I'll feel that way after I have a successful practice." In effect, they are extending and postponing their fulfillment, or waiting for permission to feel freedom and agency when they've worked hard enough.

Your Paradox will have you believe that you need to wait to feel good until you *are* good enough and deserving of it. Instead, we are going to reinvent your strategy for fueling your body with energy.

A quick note about strategy—the word.

Don't be fooled, it's not something you need an MBA to understand. Strategy is simply how you make your intention real. It's a plan, one step at a time. If you intend to work out in the morning, a strategy is to lay out your workout gear the night before, set the coffee maker to automatically make your cup of joe, and set your alarm for 6 am. Boom, strategy complete.

I have to admit, I don't like the trendy morning routines you see on social media. A thirty-year-old woman who lives in Santa Monica with her partner on the beach and who does her morning routine filled with an hour of meditation, followed by breathwork, a run on the beach, then an outdoor shower before breaking her intuitive fast at 11 am doesn't resonate with me. It's not my world, yet we often look towards people like that as experts.

Nope. Doesn't work for me. Instead, I have intentions and strategies that fit my lifestyle and how I want to live.

Here's the biggest difference a daily energetic practice will make for you: it's yours. You get to decide how you want to feel (intention) and how to make that happen (strategy). Choose the experience you are seeking and start to create that way of being now, using foundational energy-generating practices to support yourself.

*Intention + Strategy = A Life by Design*

Empires aren't built in a day; they are built day to day. It's your daily practice to be present and engaged with your mind, body, and soul to create your Clear Vision. Every moment is your opportunity to choose how you want to feel and generate your energy moment to moment.

## SELF-CARE IS THE PRACTICE OF SELF-LOVE

When you treat yourself as you would your best friend, best client, or best lover of all time—with care, respect, and gratitude—then it's like being in a loving relationship with yourself. Expanded energy grows when you love yourself, inside and out, and self-care is how you do it on a physical level.

This is your one amazing life and your one amazing body. Nourishing it with tender loving inner and outer strength-building moments will naturally expand your energy.

## Start with a Ritual Wellbeing List

I have a daily planner on paper because it's tangible, real, and gives me a place to scribble, revise, and make the declaration that "I'm done with that!" with a big fat checkmark in black sharpie next to my ritual wellbeing list. My daily ritual wellbeing list has only five things on it:

- Water
- Sleep
- Meditate
- Vitamins
- Movement

Everything else is icing on the cake.

## *Water = Flow for Energy Centers*

I love water because it loves me back. I treat myself with luxurious flavors like rose water extract, lemon and lime slices, a drop of peppermint oil to awaken my taste buds with an icy treat, or a hydrating powder for an extra boost after Zumba class. My daily Achilles' heel? La Croix. Let water nourish your skin, plump up your full, rosy cheeks, and make you more squeezable because you, my friend, are a flowing body of water.

Reinvention requires being in a relationship with your mind, body, and soul, and your mind is 80 percent water. You are 80 percent of the way to the other side of reinvention if you drink water.

Dr. Daniel Amen, author of *Feel Better Fast and Make It Last*, tells us that "being dehydrated by just 2 percent impairs your ability to carry out tasks that require attention, memory, and physical performance." He recommends eight 10-ounce glasses of water daily.

## Sleep = Intentional Rest

Arianna Huffington is the founder and CEO of Thrive Global, *The Huffington Post*, and author of about fifteen books. She wrote a book about sleep. An. Entire. Book. About. Sleep. How cool is that?

She says, "Redefining success is so important. Success has been reduced down to two metrics, money and power status, and I found in my own life, that's like sitting on a two-legged stool and sooner or later you fall off."

And she indeed fell off, knocking herself out on the corner of her desk from exhaustion.

You've probably heard that you need at least seven and a half to eight hours of sleep a night, and here's why: at approximately hour seven your brain goes through a proverbial car wash, releasing a beta-amyloid which cleans out the toxins of the previous day. This is how your brain discharges energy that is no longer needed. If you don't allow your brain to go through the car wash, you are building up toxic residues from the past, literally holding on to yesterday's energy.

The sexiest thing you can do for your wellbeing? Set a bedtime. Set an alarm to go to bed, and a wake-up time eight hours later. I have my iPhone bedtime set for 10 pm. It gives me a gentle reminder about 9:45 that it's time to go to bed, so I do. I don't think about it or question it. I pick my body up off the couch, where I was probably watching Netflix with my husband, and take my body upstairs for my nightly routine. My phone gently wakes me up at 6 am, and I make coffee and begin reading or writing. Motivated people set bedtimes because no one can sleep for you.

### *Meditation = Self-Awareness*

Five minutes, that's it. You can spare five minutes a day to sit, stand, or lie down with your eyes closed. Closing your eyes during the day is a signal to your unconscious mind that it's time to rest and recharge. I listen to ambient music, from soft twinkling bells to Buddhist monks chanting in Tibet,

## CREATE AND EXPAND YOUR ENERGY

to Amazonian birds chirping over a sprinkling waterfall. It immediately transports me out of the moment and into my crown chakra and star consciousness.

I have a small meditation space in my office. A blush pink velvet fabric drapes down from the corner of my desk into a space where I gathered a few meaningful pieces of jewelry from my grandmother's wedding day, an evil-eye glass jewel my mom brought back from Egypt, and my daughter's baptism candle. I have a sage stick which I light until it's gently smoking and, using my right hand, I swirl it around my crown chakra a few times to discharge old energy and signal my brain that it's time to relax.

Summon your sense of smell by buying a diffuser for essential oils, or, for a quick energy shift, spritz yourself with a perfume that reminds you of the beach, or your favorite season. Gift yourself a small space in your house, maybe your bedroom, or a closet (it doesn't have to be a big space) but somewhere you can call your own that is sacred and filled with small items that bring you joy.

I have a busy house, and you may too. It is filled with kids, stepkids, my husband, and two cats. I fondly refer to it as my zoo. The inner time and space you'll need to build a meditation space will be dependent on your home life. Make it yours because you are your biggest asset, and only you can gift yourself self-love. You are worthy of five minutes of inner work every day. Every. Damn. Day.

## FIND YOUR CLEAR VISION

*Vitamins = A Rainbow for Your Body*

Michelle Obama is a personal branding icon. She became First Lady, much to her chagrin, and supported her husband as well as her career, her values and beliefs, and two young girls. During this time, her Clear Vision was rooted in wellbeing. She reinvented the food pyramid into a simplified circular plate with the four food groups: fruits, vegetables, grains, and proteins—called MyPlate—as well as getting rid of high fructose sugary drinks in schools.

We've learned since grade school to "eat the rainbow" and choose foods with brighter colors—like red peppers, spinach, broccoli, and eggplants—because they have more vitamins. Nature intended for the brightness to excite our eyes and lead us towards vibrant foods from the earth.

With so many food options—organic, non-GMO, plant-based, or paleo—there is a new diet to choose from every day. You know your body best. Your one amazing body is what's going to carry your soul around for the next forty to seventy years. Honor it with delicious foods that are vitamin rich and give you energy inside and out.

How will you create energy for your vibrant future self?

How will you make it both fun and non-negotiable?

What's your first mini-step?

**CREATE AND EXPAND YOUR ENERGY**

*Movement = Medicine*

My kids have taekwondo classes every Tuesday and Thursday, and without fail, I have them in their uniforms with a bottle of water and in the car fifteen minutes before class starts. It's a non-negotiable for me (and them). I shared this with my client who was struggling with making movement a priority for her wellbeing. She has a pattern of putting everyone else's needs ahead of her own which had her not practicing a consistent workout routine, or even walking around the block after lunch because so-and-so needed her help. She realized that her wellbeing was the last thing on her list and the first thing to be crossed out in "service of others."

Here's the catch: without movement, you are limiting your impact, reducing your power, and probably feeling bloated while doing it. Like my meditation practice which started at five minutes a day, I've slowly increased my movement to support my body, and as a result, my Clear Vision has become even clearer over time. Here are a few ways you can weave movement into your day.

*Movement Mini-Steps*

Notice when you need to discharge and recharge your energy throughout your day.

I take two to three minutes to clear my energetic field at different times during the day, like in between dropping the kids off at school and beginning my workday, as well as between client sessions. I have a handful of quick movement rituals I've been practicing over the years. I can drop into a child's pose or downward-facing dog when I'm at home. Or if I'm out and about, I close my eyes and do some deep breathing, or walk around the block before my next session. I've even gone into a bathroom stall and jumped up and down to shake off excess energy before a presentation.

A client of mine sets reminders on her Apple watch to stand up and stretch every 120 minutes. She also has a macro plan for her morning routine that includes a wake-up time, workout, eating, meditation, and journaling time. This level of routine is often needed to create long-lasting rituals and habits.

## POWER PACK = PEOPLE WITH THE SAME ENERGETIC FREQUENCY

Surround yourself with people who are energetically wealthy, people who lift you and give you life, and people who believe in you and your Clear Vision. Being in a relationship with people with whom you need to radically uplevel your confidence, decision-making, and personal power will naturally raise your energetic power.

A power pack is your set of loyal people and tailored resources who believe in:

## CREATE AND EXPAND YOUR ENERGY

- intention and integrity

- action over perfection

- purpose before productivity

- creativity and intuition as guiding principles

- deep compassion and self-care

They, like you, are intentionally creating their lives and are on a journey to expand their energy to create the impossible.

### Spiritual Power Pack

Spiritual people help you grow on your Clear Vision journey. What people can support you as you form a deeper relationship with your soul? You are looking for people, places, or communities where you feel safe going within to explore your self-awareness, who you are being, and where you can reflect on spiritual works, whether that's being in meditation or forming a relationship with Source Energy, God, or the Universe.

I practice breathwork to be connected to my soul. I also have a personal consciousness guide and lightworker I meet with monthly. My family and I attend an open-minded and activist-driven church in the West Loop neighborhood of Chicago.

People whom you admire for their positive energy, who replenish and inspire you, are also part of your spiritual power pack. For instance, I include Gabrielle Bernstein, author of *Super Attractor*, and Danielle LaPorte, author of T*he Desire Map*, in my Power Pack. Think about who and what lights up your inner spirit, and put their energy in your spiritual power pack.

## Emotional Power Pack

These are people that are always there for you when you need to pop. When you are around them, they will generate massive energy for you by holding space for all of your emotional needs. They can be friends, your family of choice, support groups like AA, or a virtual community. These are your coaches and therapists. Your emotional power pack offers empathy, constructive support, and compassion without judgment.

## Community Power Pack

These are the groups of people you surround yourself with. They can be paid communities; for example, I've been a member and columnist for the American Marketing Association, and I've also been a member at Soho House in Chicago. Choose communities that light you up and empower you.

If you can't find the community you desire, create it. In 2013 I co-founded Forth Chicago, which was a community for creative entrepreneurs. I saw there was a gap missing in communities, for creative professional women, and I wanted to be around this type of energy, so Julie Schumacher, Kelly Allison, and I created it. In 2021 I created the Clear Vision U program to support ambitious people who are at a major transition in their personal and professional life. Being in community helps you remember you aren't alone.

## Fitness Power Pack

Find one or two supportive friends who are into fitness, working out, walking, or whatever it is for you. In my power pack, I have my seventy-plus-year-old mom who goes to her local gym for strength training and walks three miles a day on her "day off." I also have my sister who is a lawyer, RN, mother, and a dance instructor. Whenever I have a productive workout, I text them, simply to let them know that "Hey, I went to Zumba today and it was so fun!"

## Accountability Power Pack

These are people you hire to hold you accountable. A friend will let you off the hook when life gets hard, a spiritual person may let your feelings get the best of you, but an accountability partner will help you focus on results. Oftentimes these are people you pay to push you. Think of a fitness trainer, leadership coach, or results coach. They are invested in your vision.

## FIND YOUR CLEAR VISION

Every good coach has their own coach. In addition to having a business coach and personal consciousness guide, I do a weekly check-in with my coaching community. These non-negotiables hold me accountable to the future-forward person I want to be.

Accountability is the linchpin to ground you into consistently measured growth.

Leaders don't do it alone. Building a power pack will lift you up, in turn helping expand your energy to make clear decisions that will not only elevate your personal power, but the impact that you make in your world and the lives of others. Who will you ask for support? Who will be in your power pack? A life coach, leadership coach, or personal trainer?

Call them, text them, and book it today.

As I said, there are those who create energy and those who drain it. Managing, discharging, and recharging your energetic sources will give you power to create the impossible, open you up to possibilities beyond what is currently available, and pop you into your Clear Vision daily.

Your inner world is waiting to be nourished with replenishing flowing energy up and down the eight energetic centers of your body. Gift yourself the time, space, and people to uplift your mind, body, and soul through intentional energetic work. Even if you are starting with taking your daily vitamins

## CREATE AND EXPAND YOUR ENERGY

and getting to sleep before midnight, it's a start on your path toward who you are becoming. Your future self will thank you—trust me!

Now that you have the foundation to source infinite energy, it's time to expand your inner trust.

# Chapter 8

# TRUST YOUR NEW IDENTITY

Everything changed for Meera when she said, "If I'm being honest…"

Meera was a senior leader at a well-known tech company. She had been working towards this role for years. Her boss had recently left, and she was now leading a team of sixty international employees and working twelve-hour days with hopes that it would set her up to be partner soon.

Meera's dropbox way of being was to spend her days in a Superwoman Paradox Pattern, saying "yes" to things when she should have been saying "no," and swooping in to "save the day." She was in effect telling her subconscious that she couldn't show any sign of weakness, and if she did, the team would fall apart, she'd have to work late, not work out, and basically be unhappy.

Underneath, she felt fearful and vulnerable because she knew she was on the verge of burnout and no longer had the pizazz that originally led her to this work in the first place. Nonetheless, she kept telling herself she had to stick it out until she made partner because then she would be happy.

In our session, I asked her to complete the sentence stem, "If I'm being honest…" and honesty spilled out of her in words and tears.

"I shouldn't have to work this hard.

I don't want to manage sixty people.

I haven't worked out in weeks. I'm dead tired.

I'm not paid enough to do this shit.

I want time off."

When we aren't connected to our truth, we think "this is the way it is," especially within a career we've worked so long and hard to create. Being truthful with how you feel and what you want is the first step to connect with your pop energy and your most vibrant self, who is being honest all the time; if only we would listen a little more closely.

Meera didn't fly off the handle and share her most inner thoughts with her team or a co-worker, but after exploring different options, she walked into HR and shared, "If I'm being honest, I want time off. Unpaid for two months."

And they said okay.

Meera started to be honest in other areas of her life, like in her relationship with her partner, and most importantly with herself. She implemented a new pattern of being honest, which opened up new opportunities and led to clear communication.

## TRUSTING IS MESSY WORK

*Honesty + Trust = Clear Communication*

### Trusting Ourselves Is Messy Work

We've been taught not to trust our decisions:

"Don't jump to any conclusions."

"Are you sure about that?"

"I don't know, I can't decide."

### Trusting Others Is Messy Work

Our Paradox cultivates mistrust by making us feel inadequate and doubtful. When someone is being too nice, we think, "What do they really want?"

## TRUST YOUR NEW IDENTITY

Or when something goes right, we think, "Wait, that never happens."

Or when someone praises you, you ask, "Don't they know me?", and you start to doubt your ability to trust them because if they really knew you, they'd know that you aren't that good. Their positive feedback contrasts with your Paradox, who doesn't believe you are good enough for that big promotion, new client, or worthy of love.

Distrust often stems from early childhood. Maybe you were manipulated or abused and you learned it was not safe to trust others. Your relationship to trust may have stemmed from how you were raised and the cultural influences you were taught, or maybe you are a child of divorce, what many people call a "broken" home, and that created ideas of whom to trust and whom not to.

Maybe you had a mean older brother or neighbor who told all of your secrets, and you were constantly afraid of being hurt so you would shield your trust and hide your secrets as a form of self-protection because you felt ashamed.

Distrust bleeds into romantic relationships in the form of jealousy, like being overprotective, in fear they will leave you. Or you go to the opposite end of the spectrum and avoid commitment altogether because you are afraid of getting hurt, or figure "it's just not worth the pain."

## FIND YOUR CLEAR VISION

### Trusting "The Man" Is Super Messy Work

Breeding distrust has been a patriarchal and media strategy for decades. We've inherited a capitalist patriarchal model of leadership where ambition and a do-it-yourself attitude are glorified. The masculine energy to survive by all means necessary—to protect you and yours, and to constantly compete—breeds distrust.

Society is built on outdated obligations to be a certain way, which mutes outliers and individualism, particularly as it relates to feelings and trust. There are consequences for crying at work. For example, you are labeled as "emotional." Or consider the age-old stereotype of an ambitious woman being "bitchy."

So we downplay our feelings, and ruminate in our heads over "Why do I feel this way? What's wrong with me?"

With so many different media messages based on fear, lack, and survival, it's no wonder we are wobbly when it comes to trusting ourselves and others.

Let's look at the opposite scenario. What would it look like to trust ourselves? To collectively embody trust, faith, and understanding that our best interest is being expressed with heart? What if it was safe to trust yourself? What if you were indeed safe to fully express how you feel? And, if you are being honest, doesn't it feel great to do so?

## TRUST YOUR NEW IDENTITY

Releasing how trust has gone for you in the past will open up the gateway to a new pattern of inner trust based on self-worth, connection, and humanity.

## THE DRAMA TRIANGLE REINVENTED

Creativity loves to play. It ebbs and flows with recharging energy, bouncing between a problem to be solved and all the ways to do it. Creativity relishes in the unknown.

Inner trust is knowing that who you are is more than enough to live without knowing the right answer and without knowing the outcome. Instead, you are worthy of clarity in who you are being, and trusting yourself becomes an everyday experience.

Let's choose to trust. Here's how. Being rooted in trust, self-worth, and valuing your creativity are core pillars of the Inner Platform.

## CREATOR CONSCIOUSNESS ENERGY

Your Creator Consciousness Energy rises above the Drama Triangle, which has you busy bouncing between the victim, rescuer, and abuser, past the Anti-Creator Consciousness, which has you sacrificing yourself, or at war with others because of your righteous thinking. No longer tied to repeating patterns of lower-level consciousness, the Creator designs their own reality by practicing self-worth energy, connection energy, and human collective energy. But, to get there,

# FIND YOUR CLEAR VISION

we need to unhook from the embedded stories and power dynamics that our subconscious has been looping forever.

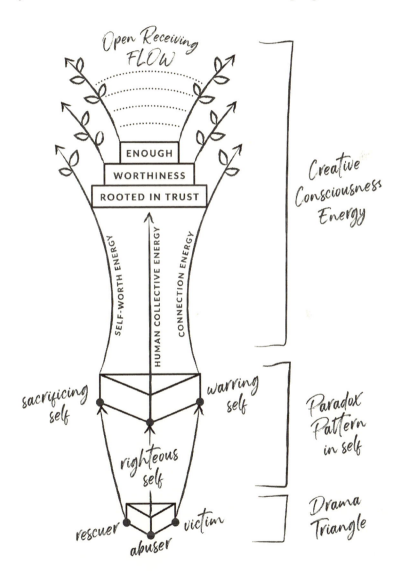

## TRUST YOUR NEW IDENTITY

This model is how you can receive creative flow when you are fully connected to your most vibrant self, others, and humanity. You are only open to receiving as much as you are willing to give. The openness between Creator Consciousness Energy and your most vibrant self is the pathway to flow and creativity.

### How Do You Get Started?

Life gives you opportunities to practice Creator Consciousness thinking every day. An experience will present itself, and you have the opportunity to create an imagined future experience from whom you want to be, fully connected to yourself, others, and humanity. Or you can choose a future experience from righteousness, war, and sacrifice. Making choices from the pop will increase your capacity to continue to reinvent. It will connect you to a greater capacity of energy and inner trust.

Choosing from distrust and a closed mindset will lead to more of the same: incremental changes, but no real transformation. It's an inner power struggle to protect who you are but doesn't leave room for growth. Funny enough, you are growing when you are most uncomfortable.

Choosing from inner trust will build self-awareness and awaken the divine feminine traits of aliveness, creativity, flow, collaboration, and connection.

## Replace the Sacrificing Self with Self-Worth Energy

Searching for your own worthiness in others is a lose-lose game.

The Sacrificing Self lives in a loop of serving others, which is fine, if you could drop the shame, guilt, and remorse for not doing more, basically beating yourself up in the process of caring so much.

To elevate out of sacrificing energy to self-worth energy, the Sacrificing Self will need to make it a priority to be worthy of their own love and attention by saying "no" to things that aren't aligned with their vision, because they are worthy of love without doing anything.

When you say "no" for the first time, pause and place a hand on your heart and gently tap it a few times to the beat of your heart to remind you of your presence and worthiness to make choices that are a "Hell yes" for you.

## Replace Your Warring Self with Connection Energy

Oftentimes the thing that annoys us about someone else is the thing that we need to confront within ourselves. This is how jealousy works, for example. When you are jealous of someone, there is something within you that you are unwilling to look at, so you avoid it by armoring up with layers of

## TRUST YOUR NEW IDENTITY

self-protection, disconnection, and distrust to avoid uncomfortable feelings.

To unhook from your Warring Self and align with your Connection Energy, you need to be with your own insecurities.

There is more than enough energy, time, space, love, you name it, to go around, and choosing to be with your own insecurities, rather than pushing them away, will create connection to yourself and others.

A visual practice to remind yourself of connection energy is to weave your fingers together as if you are holding your own hand with fingers intertwined. Raise and lower your intertwined fingers a few times and imagine that it's the weaving together of connection between you and others. Just as each finger on your hand is a different size and shape—some have tiny scars from your past—each human in our world has a different experience we can connect to. There is more than enough energy for everyone in the world.

### Replace Your Righteous Self with Connection to Humanity

Just think of all of the bright ideas you are missing when you are busy being right.

Fighting for what's "right" (remember, only your logic is logical) disconnects you from what's possible in your life, livelihood, and relationships. Instead, unhook from the need to "know" and practice listening with your ears wide open. The world isn't so black and white. It is a colorful rainbow of insights and opportunities if you open your eyes to see them.

When you feel your righteous energy, imagine you have a pair of dark sunglasses on, and when you take them off, a full spectrum of color appears before you. Sit with all of the colors of the world before you say a word or declare yourself right and someone else wrong. There are many versions of what's right and wrong, seeing a colorful world before you will connect you to your creativity.

In order to have peace, you must be peaceful.

In order to have love, you must be loving.

In order to trust, you must be trusting.

In order to create, you must be the creator.

You get to choose how you want to show up and be in these moments. Choose wisely from what feelings you want to magnetically attract. Trust is a practice to stretch into, aspire to hold within your being, and shine out. As you practice inner trust, it shines out to others to inspire them and results in your being someone who is trustworthy.

## TRUST YOUR NEW IDENTITY

## "I GET SO NERVOUS, WHAT SHOULD I DO?"

My client was growing her healthcare business and was asked to be a guest on a series of podcast interviews. Her know-it-all Paradox Pattern wanted her to know all of the questions in advance, which sucked the fun out of the conversation and had her worried she wasn't going to clearly communicate, making her sound like a dunce.

She shared with me that her need to know it all stemmed from a Toastmasters speech she had given years before when she tried to talk without her notes, but her brain went blank and she froze. She was mortified. Her Paradox shared all the reasons why this podcast series wasn't going to be fun: "I'm going to stumble over my words and bomb these interviews. No one will think I'm an expert—it's going to be awful." She continued to collect evidence that it was going to be uncomfortable and to paint herself as a fool.

Her Paradox wanted to research for hours to get ready for the interviews, but deep down she knew it would come out rehearsed and wouldn't sound authentic.

She didn't trust herself because her mind played tricks on her.

Overly ambitious people often over-prepare. Sound familiar? I asked her to take her level of preparedness and need to know everything from 200 percent to 75 percent. It was out of her comfort zone.

**FIND YOUR CLEAR VISION**

At the end of the session, she agreed to take her over-preparing and anxiety down to a 75 percent experience, and block out ten minutes before the podcast to clear her mind, do a quick meditation, and a few stretches.

She wanted to use the affirmation: "I'm willing to practice trusting myself."

"What??" I replied, "Willing to practice?"

This is like dipping your toe into the pool of trusting yourself and thinking you are swimming laps.

Being willing to do something is alerting your subconscious that you are open to the idea—that's it.

She was preparing to fail. Here's what I mean:

Preparing to fail sounds like:

"This won't be too hard."

"I won't fumble through this."

"I'm not so bad."

Saying these things is a non-starter; you're alerting your subconscious mind to create a lukewarm experience.

## TRUST YOUR NEW IDENTITY

Lukewarm language is an energetically low way to trust your most vibrant self. To continue with the swimming metaphor, you've got your swimsuit on and are willing to go into the pool, telling yourself "it's not too cool." But on the inside, you are hanging on for dear life—you've already started bracing yourself to freeze, sealing off your lungs from the shock, your hands are gripped tightly at your sides, your heart racing as you begin to jump up and down in order to generate heat in advance of jumping into the pool. Your energy level has aligned with freezing, and all of your thoughts and actions are going towards it.

So instead, you'll sit in the car with your suit on, stewing over why you put yourself in these situations in the first place.

Be cautious of using language that is half-baked and keeps you moving forward at a snail's pace of limited possibility. That's not the game you are playing. You are attracting higher-level thoughts aligned with your Clear Vision to create your life by design and fully connected to the language of creativity and possibility.

Get your suit on, walk to the edge of the pool, and dive in!

Everyone is practicing this game called life, wholeheartedly trusting themselves to show up with clarity, stumble through it if necessary, and do it again. That's what visionary people do.

I asked my client to write down "I trust myself." She wrote it once, scribbled it out, wrote it again with handwriting that looked like a second-grader, as if her know-it-all Paradox was trying to prove to her that she didn't even know how to spell *trust*.

We were now in a deep conversation with her Paradox, who wanted to protect her from looking foolish or making a mistake, which is its job and something we could acknowledge it for.

Your inner world, the language you speak to yourself, trusting yourself (or not), all reflect in your outer expression. Notice the automatic talk that flows from Paradox:

"I don't know how to do this."

"I have to do it all myself."

"I'll never get this right."

When speaking in this manner, your Paradox has a stronghold on your future by altering your subconscious mind that life is indeed hard, so plan accordingly. You can't keep promises. See? You just broke one!

The Paradox will set out to prove you right or wrong based on your thoughts. And use language to keep you trapped.

Instead, use subtle language shifts to play a different game—language that builds in some wiggle room to get creative with how life is going to go from a place of "let's try this on for size."

# TRUST YOUR NEW IDENTITY

The word "can't" is a paradoxical paradise. It's a stopping point that alerts your subconscious mind that whatever task or decision is in front of you is impossible and we're going to stop you right there.

"I can't ask for that."

"I can't make it tonight."

"We can't go after that project."

Notice that after "can't" is often your logical reasoning why not.

"I can't ask for that because I don't have an MBA."

"I can't make it tonight because I have too much work to do."

"We can't go after that project because we don't have the experience."

The first level of moving from paradoxical language to clear communication is to take responsibility for who you are being.

## WHAT TO SAY

Choose words you desire instead of what you want to avoid. For example:

"I don't know how to do this," but add the three-letter word "yet."

I don't know how to do this...YET.

Let's try it on:

"I don't know how to swim yet."

"I don't know my Clear Vision yet."

"I don't have a partner yet."

Give your most vibrant self your full trust, adoration, and a "you've got this, sister!" attitude. Flood her with the space to play, practice, and experiment. Communicate with her as you would a friend because talking with your new BFF—your most vibrant self—is the first step towards being in a relationship with her.

My client continued to write the affirmation "I trust myself," which awoke her intuition, carving out space for compassion, play, and belief in herself. And she went into the podcast interviews with confidence and nailed it—ten out of ten!

## TRUST YOUR NEW IDENTITY

> **BRIGHT TOOL:**
> **CREATIVE PLAN FOR INNER TRUST:**
>
> **Release Judgment** using this self-affirming mantra: "I'm okay not knowing. I am worthy, more than enough, and rooted in trust. I am open to receiving flow."
>
> **Brainstorm** how to practice trust today. Maybe there are decisions to be made at work, or you need to express yourself to your partner and ask for what you need. Jot down two to three places you can practice trusting yourself.
>
> **Laser Focus:** Tell yourself, "It's safe to trust myself and my choices." See where that feeling lands in your body, and if there is unease, ask yourself, "Am I willing to love myself enough to let that feeling go?"
>
> **Roadmap:** Where, this week, can you practice trusting yourself?
>
> **Share:** Who will you share your journey with?

Trusting yourself can be messy, at first. It takes honesty, practice, and courage to say and do the bold thing that's in alignment with who you are becoming on your Clear Vision journey. Will you belly flop into the pool once or twice? Sure, we all do. But, trusting your new identity—your most vibrant

## FIND YOUR CLEAR VISION

self—will propel you forward in your decision-making, personal growth, and confidence to dry yourself off and jump back in.

Now, with your swimsuit on, ready to dive headfirst into trust, let's get into flow.

Chapter 9

# CHOOSE FLOW ON PURPOSE

My family and I were on a canoe trip on the Mexico and United States border. We were supposed to launch the canoes into the Rio Grande about three miles from our destination, but African Killer Bees had become a recent problem at the launch pad, so we had to put our canoes another two miles downriver.

I wasn't worried about the two additional miles tacked on to the afternoon. I had it made, because in my canoe, I had my two-time varsity athlete stepson with me. Being overly competitive and overly confident people, we declared that we would lead the other canoes up the river.

I was in the back at the helm, steering the canoe, and my stepson was in the front, paddling as fast as he could. To steer a canoe, you tilt your paddle in the water in the direction you want to go. Tilt towards the left, the boat goes left. Tilt your paddle right, the boat goes right.

## CHOOSE FLOW ON PURPOSE

Ten minutes into our trip, I couldn't get the hang of it. I would tip the paddle in the water too much, overcorrecting the canoe which led us to the Mexican side of the river, and then I would overcorrect and lead us back to the US side. From a bird's-eye view, you could see us zig-zagging back and forth across the Rio Grande, getting nowhere fast.

The other canoes flowed past us with little effort. My sister threw me a knowing smile that she was going to beat us. *Dammit!* It took us an extra forty-five minutes to get to the landing pad. My arms were sore, I was sweating like crazy, and obviously not cut out for water sports.

The zig-zag of plotting, over-correcting, and expending time and energy eventually landed us in the same spot as the rest of the family, but they expended zero energy, and we had a red-hot sunburn.

We weren't in flow. Sometimes you zig-zag from one extreme to the other, back and forth across the Rio Grande. Sometimes the dizzying zig-zag is happening in your mind, and time, energy, and confidence are lost in the commotion.

How do you find flow and stay in it? Matthew McConaughey says, "It takes a lot of effort to be this relaxed." It takes a lot of mind power to go with the flow. What if I dipped my paddle into the water a little less, what if we didn't paddle as if our lives depended on it just to beat my sister? What if we just simply and literally went with the flow?

## FIND YOUR CLEAR VISION

Flow asks us to be willing to detach from the outcome. We could have floated downriver and probably made it to our location, no problem, but my pride and competitiveness got in the way, blocking me from the flow.

Flow doesn't ask you to do anything; it particularly doesn't ask you to overdo it. Notice when you are over-anything: over-correcting, overthinking, overdoing, overachieving, overwhelming…you aren't connected to your vibrant self, and you certainly aren't in flow.

Imagine that your boss assigns you to a new client project. You immediately start to question, "How long is this going to take? Remember last time? I was here all weekend. How am I going to get this done when I have so much else to do?"

Your mind goes wild thinking of all the reasons this is going to bump into your weekend plans, and it's only Tuesday. Your mind throws you into a self-induced state of overthinking about how this type of situation has gone in the past, and you spend precious time and energy predicting the future in your mind. You're no longer grounded at the moment. Instead, you've created scenarios of "how come?" and "why me?"

When presented with an unknown experience, the mind fills in the blanks, but it's pulling on energy from the past, it's tainted energy that tells the mind "We've seen this movie, we know the ending, and it ain't pretty." Your unwillingness to be with a new experience blocks flow from entering the room.

## CHOOSE FLOW ON PURPOSE

Dr. David Hawkins was the director of The Institute for Spiritual Research, Inc. He was a pioneer researcher in the field of consciousness. He spent his lifetime creating tools of consciousness, measuring the frequency and vibration of energy within our bodies to help human beings learn how to create their happiness, and flow, from within.

His Map of Consciousness, similar to the Abraham-Hicks Emotional Scale, makes understanding our mindset easy: negative emotions are destructive, and positive emotions are creative.

**CREATIVE (RECHARGING) ENERGY**

Enlightenment

Peace

Freedom

Joy

Love

Acceptance

Willingness

Neutral

Courage

> **DESTRUCTIVE (DISCHARGING) ENERGY**
>
> Pride
>
> Anger
>
> Worry
>
> Grief
>
> Guilt
>
> Shame
>
> Despair

Simply put, Dr. Hawkins said, "Love heals, fear constricts."

Let's try this concept on. Fold a piece of paper in half. On one side of the paper write "My mind tells me" and on the other side write "My heart tells me."

Think about an upcoming experience that you are nervous about, something you think may not go your way, or won't go as planned. Get into the victim side of these emotions on purpose. Pull up the low-level feelings so we can play with them.

Under "My mind tells me," write down all of the negative and nasty ways this future experience will turn out. Pour it out. Be sad and disappointed on purpose and really get into the depths of your victim mentality. It won't feel good and you may start to laugh at yourself, because, yes, it's silly to see the thoughts and emotions you have been telling yourself in your head written down in real time. Your Paradox loves to mess with your feelings by crafting stories of why things never go your way.

Once complete, close your eyes to recenter and take a few deep cleansing breaths to release that lower-level energy. Move into what your heart tells you about the upcoming experience and pour out all of the thoughts and feelings of what *could* happen when you listen to your heart.

My heart tells me...

"It's going to be okay."

"Let's try it out."

"I believe in you."

"It will be fun!"

"You've got this!"

Notice the difference in energy between what your mind versus your heart has to say about an experience that hasn't even happened yet. Who would you rather listen to? Who are you going to trust? Who speaks kindly to you and has your back?

## FIND YOUR CLEAR VISION

Practice flow with others:

- Let everyone merge ahead of you on the highway.

- Say hello to everyone at your local bodega.

- Smile at people you see on the street.

Connecting to other people's energy will increase your capacity to flow.

Ask yourself, "How do I want to feel at the end of the day?"

When an experience occurs, a thought will follow it. Ask yourself, "Is this thought draining me of energy or creating energy? You'll receive a quick "Yes" or "No" from your body, and shift accordingly.

Continue to choose from creative versus destructive energy, and zig and zag until you stay popped longer. There's no right or wrong way to flow, but the easiest way is to let go of the inner resistance of thinking you "know" how it's going to go.

Creativity loves novelty; it sparks ideas. Try on something new to create and spark flow.

Buy something new from the grocery store you've never tried before. Dragon fruit, anyone?

## CHOOSE FLOW ON PURPOSE

Join a sports team with no experience.

Join an exotic dance class.

Write a poem.

Subscribe to a coffee of the month club.

Canoe the Rio Grande.

You may think, "Lisa, buy dragon fruit? Really? I don't have the confidence that this is going to give me flow."

You don't need confidence to flow. Confidence is a paradoxical strategy to "get ready."

What you need to pop into any creative mindset are courage and commitment. Not confidence.

Courage is the energetic level of empowerment that's needed right before you do a hard thing.

*Courage + Commitment = Confidence*

You already have courage. Think back to a time when you were young, sometime between fourth grade and junior high school when you were proud of something you did. Maybe you stood up to a bully, dove off the high dive, ran for student council, participated in your school's talent show. Picture that thing you did in your mind.

## FIND YOUR CLEAR VISION

How did you feel before you did that thing? Nervous, scared, maybe felt like you were having an out-of-body experience? Feel it in your body right now, and put yourself in that memory right before you did the thing.

After you did the thing, what feelings were you left with? Excitement! Inner pride! Elation! An "I can do anything!" feeling! Your heart is glowing, your breath is fueled, your blood is pumping. You feel alive!

Confidence comes after you do the thing. Choose a positive, empowered feeling from your past and let your body's natural reaction flow through you.

Imagine your most vibrant self, a year from now when you are living with courage. You are managing and expanding your energy, and living in authentic expression to your greatest potential. Trust that who you were in the past, as that fourth-grader, or as the high school freshman, has led you to who you are today. You can stretch and expand, wiggle, and throw yourself into courageous moments. The flow is inside of you.

Release resistance. Replenish your courage.

Here's the thing about flow: it's an action. Flow is not something to be inspired by; it's in the doing that you create flow. You are the inspiration, the vessel for creativity.

Just like you can't be a writer and have writer's block.

## CHOOSE FLOW ON PURPOSE

You can't be a swimmer if you never get in the pool.

You can't be a visionary without a vision.

You can't be a thought leader without thoughts and leadership.

You are bringing together dueling energies. It's no wonder change often looks so small; it's trapped in its resistance to higher-level energy. We are not making change; we are creating transformation, which begins when you start.

Generating flow on purpose creates agency in your life. You master this creative process and you, my friend, are a self-aware guru.

Your clear overflowing mindset is what dreams are made of. You have the golden ticket; you have the creative flow.

Trust your most vibrant self. You have the power and personal energy to help you shine bright with the confidence you've been waiting for. Now, with your Inner Platform built and you have the tools to flip the switch from drop to pop, it's time to move into the Outer Platform, the expression of who you are in the world transformed.

# Part III

# YOUR OUTER PLATFORM

*"Paint a picture of the future with your idea in it."*

–TOM KELLEY

# Chapter 10

# YOUR OUTER PLATFORM

IN 2008, I WAS ONE OF THE FIRST PEOPLE TO SIGN UP for Gwyneth Paltrow's newsletter where she shared new-age practices she was trying—like cupping and vaginal steaming. My voyeuristic mind was so curious. "What in the world!? What is that?! Where can I get one of those?"

Before Goop became the lifestyle brand it is today with multiple product lines from vitamins to vibrators, it was a newsletter of GP's quirky things she'd try. Led by her curiosity and intuition, she would try new things and share consistently in this newsletter. Mainstream media shunned her for her holiday gift guide with a $1,000 gold-plated juicer, as well as when she Consciously Uncoupled from her husband, Coldplay's front man, Chris Martin, in 2014.

But here's the thing—she was led by her curiosity and shared. And did it again and again, effectively building her target audience and positioning herself as the godmother of the wellness industry.

Did anyone buy the $1,000 gold-plated juicer? Who cares? She continued to show up and was laughing all the way to the bank.

What is your gold-plated juicer?

It's your Clear Vision. Sharing your Clear Vision is the next step in your reinvention, and it's what makes you visionary. Becoming a visionary person is transforming what was previously impossible into possible and making it real. You have the vision; now we make it real using the Outer Platform Framework.

Let's put it another way. There's a distinct difference between being a thought leader and a philosopher: philosophers think, and thought leaders think *and* lead.

Thought leaders are highly recognized in their field of expertise because they think of and share new ways of thinking and working. True thought leaders are visionary people. The difference between a leader and a thought leader is that thought leaders are also brands because they strategically amplify themselves as an authority in their industry.

Just because you have a Clear Vision doesn't make you visionary. Taking inspired action by making your idea come to life—through who you are being and what you are doing—makes you visionary.

**FIND YOUR CLEAR VISION**

Don't get me wrong—you can have a Clear Vision and not share; many artists do this. They live within a thriving inner world filled with creativity and imagination, painting masterpieces every week. But we aren't artists; we are creative leaders—living and breathing embodiments of our vision—who want to make a bigger and lasting impact. It is who you are, day in and day out. And now we share.

So, where do you start? Lucky for you, you already have.

Do you have a LinkedIn account? Then you have a professional brand.

Do you have a career? Then you have a professional brand.

Do you have an Instagram account? Then you have a personal brand.

Do you have a mission that you believe in? Then you have a personal brand.

You get the picture—you have a brand.

Your personal and professional brand is alive and kicking on LinkedIn, Google, or Instagram. Go ahead and Google yourself. You can see what life your brand has taken on if you haven't been creating it with intention.

A personal brand is an exchange of energy between you and your audience. Your audience sees, feels, and remembers your presence, personality, and reputation because you intentionally nurture and nourish the relationship through storytelling, visual presence, and messaging.

Think of most actors and actresses.

Think of Anderson Cooper or any news anchor.

Think of almost any professional athlete.

Think of Britain's Royal family.

Their outward appearance looks so natural, yet it's polished and oftentimes very calculated in how they present themselves to their audience to keep their career on an upward trajectory.

A professional brand will communicate who you are in your workplace, industry, and future professional life. A Clear Vision can be both personal and professional; it's how you execute the storytelling, visual presence, and messaging that will make the difference.

Chances are I'm not telling you anything new. You've seen personal and professional brands in action. So, the question is, how do you build an effective personal or professional brand?

The Outer Platform Framework will teach you how to express who you are in the world outside of yourself; it's how you show

## FIND YOUR CLEAR VISION

Taking inspired action, collaborating, and building your personal or professional brand is all the more important today because social media plays such a vital role in our lives. People are influencing our thinking, purchasing, and values. We need to choose wisely who we give our attention, money, and likes to.

Humanity is torn between left and right politics. Cancel culture and social media have put enormous pressure on everyone. Your Paradox will have you believe the worst-case scenario—that you'll be judged, or you will be overlooked, which will only perpetuate your Paradox, effectively canceling yourself before you even start.

The length of time it takes you to build your Outer Platform doesn't make your Clear Vision any less valid, or you any less committed to its outcome. Instead, life's adversities and U-turns are how you will practice staying anchored and in integrity with your vision.

Anyone can learn how to execute the best ad campaign out there, buy followers, or buy their way onto a board or panel. People can talk so loudly that others have to hear them, but true creative expression is seen, felt, and remembered by those that need to hear it—your people and your audience.

When building a personal brand, many traditional brand strategists or marketing agencies will start with the strategy—the how to get it done and blanket the internet with you. That no longer works.

I do it differently, and here's why: personal and professional branding is a mindset and an exchange of energy. Your brand is who you are, the energy you bring into a room, the stories you tell, and the relationships you nurture, and how your audience feels when you leave the room. Marketing, on the other hand, is "how" you showcase and build awareness of your brand.

In order to create a visionary brand, you need to be in the pop—a brand that lights you up and is playing full out to win the game of reinvention: being you in every way. When you are sharing your Clear Vision, making choices that are aligned with it, and trusting yourself, you are naturally more open to receiving creative downloads, new ideas, and opportunities, which results in career advancement. Watch how this unfolds.

## BE WHO YOU ARE ON PURPOSE, WITH PURPOSE

When you have a Clear Vision and you know what aspirational success looks like for you and why it's important, then you become a visionary leader, someone who expresses their vision through inspired action. This results in elevating your expertise. **Visionary leaders have a Clear Vision.**

When you trust yourself and your decisions, you become trustworthy. A trustworthy person actively listens and creates genuine connections. Presence shows up with ease because you believe in your value. You trust yourself being in the flow of the unknown, yet anchored in self-worth. Visionaries are naturally adaptable and in integrity with their word, which results in advancing their career. **Trustworthy people trust themselves.**

When your mind is aligned with your most vibrant self, you are self-aware, which results in confidence, presence, and creativity. Confidence is naturally embedded into your brand when you've done the Inner Platform work to know who you are without the clutter of "who you should be." Creative people naturally have an authentic voice and message. **Creative people are self-aware.**

When you expand your energy through rituals and habits that support your most vibrant self, you model transformational leadership through transparency, executive presence, and the language you use to express yourself. Your ideas are clear and your intention is transparent because you are connected to yourself and others through the Creator Consciousness that is within everyone. This results in you becoming who you are meant to be: **the most vibrant version of yourself.**

You have all the ingredients to build your Outer Platform because you've done the inner work.

## INNER TO OUTER PLATFORM MODEL

Download the Inner to Outer Platform Model at:
www.bebrightlisa.com/findyourclearvision-book

## YOUR OUTER PLATFORM

| INNER PLATFORM | | OUTER PLATFORM |
|---|---|---|
| **INNER TRUST**<br>Trust yourself<br>and your decisions<br>**RESILIENT** |  | **TRUSTWORTHY**<br>Active listening, adaptability and<br>integrity creates genuine connection<br>*career advancement* |
| **MINDSET**<br>Be in a relationship with<br>your most vibrant self<br>**SELF-AWARENESS** |  | **CREATIVITY**<br>Self-awareness, confidence,<br>and executive presence<br>*authentic voice & message* |
| **EXPANDED ENERGY**<br>Rituals and habits to<br>expand personal energy<br>**INSPIRATIONAL** |  | **CLEAR COMMUNICATION**<br>Model transformational leadership through<br>messaging, motivation and transparency<br>*transformational leader* |
| **CLEAR VISION**<br>Clarify your future vision and<br>what success looks like<br>**CONFIDENCE** | → | **VISIONARY LEADER**<br>Express your Clear Vision<br>through inspired action<br>*elevated expertise* |

## The M Word: Marketing

Personal branding is the energy you bring to building stories, memories, and relationships. It's adding consistent value and building trust with your audience.

Marketing, on the other hand, is all about the "how." How are you going to showcase your personal brand to the world and in what ways? It's about sharing. That's it. It doesn't have to be selling, sales, and slimy messaging to convince someone you are the right person for the job; you simply share who you are and what you're all about.

Branding is about building personality. This is why we are attracted to certain brands; they remind us of our values. Say you want to buy a new pair of black leggings to work out in. Some people would call these "yoga pants" and buy them from Lululemon for over $100 because Lululemon's values and brand identity aligns with who they want to be seen as, and sure, maybe they like the fit of the yoga pants and their butt looks amazing in them.

Similarly, someone may head down to the local Walgreens and buy a pair of black leggings they have in a box next to the chips and dip for $10 after the New Year when they are promoting "New Year, New You."

Both pairs of leggings provide the same functionality—they are black leggings to work out in. One represents luxury, eco-friendly sustainability, and thread count. The other represents convenience and a thrifty value. Both are examples of how different personalities buy for different reasons.

Brand marketing is how you build brand awareness. Lululemon has spent incredible amounts of money building brand

## YOUR OUTER PLATFORM

awareness through strategic partnerships with local fitness instructors and studios. They give discounts to their brand ambassadors to buy and wear their products. And they have workout events in-store to bring the audience right to the cash register. They have positioned their brand in between Nike, an athletic brand, and Victoria's Secret PINK, a trendy fashion brand, to market to a distinct audience who is willing to pay big bucks for black leggings.

Now, here's the shift from big business branding to you.

Instead of building a brand personality (which is a one-way conversation), personal branding is an exchange of energy, from you to others. Personal marketing is how you authentically share your energy.

Like Lululemon uses traditional branding techniques to build awareness, a personal brand touches someone through storytelling, visual presence, and messaging which happens in what designers call brand touchpoints. These include any platform where you touch your customers, clients, or potential employers like your LinkedIn page, a personal website, social media channels, a thank-you note, an email signature, and your leadership.

It takes between seven and twenty-seven times for someone to be touched by your brand before they feel that they know, like, and trust you. We used to be able to get away with slapping our resumes on LinkedIn, adding a profile picture, and occasionally posting an article or two that we liked, but, let's be honest, we probably didn't read it, and neither did anyone else. Nowadays, to make the impact we desire, creating a personal brand encompasses much more.

A fully expressed personal brand is a series of ongoing conversations, both visual and verbal, which come together to create a brand experience.

A personal or professional brand isn't a one-way conversation, or a "build it and they will come." It's a way of being. It's who you are. Your Outer Platform doesn't require a marketing team; it requires your commitment to cultivating how you show up every day as someone committed to your vision.

Think of the Outer Platform as a garden, one that needs tending to, but doesn't bloom just because you watered it once last month. It requires attention, sunshine, and regular watering. It requires time and patience as you weed out disempowering paradoxical thoughts and you expand your Inner Platform to be in flow with whatever life is going to throw your way.

Talk to plants and they will grow. Talk with humans and they will too.

## Positioning of Your Outer Platform

What is brand positioning and why is it important for personal and professional branding?

## YOUR OUTER PLATFORM

A business brand wants to leave a lasting impression in the mind of the customer, so that a customer knows, likes, and trusts them. To do that they use a strategy called brand positioning which crystallizes the benefits and objectives of the brand, and who the brand is targeting. Once the brand is positioned against the marketplace with clear benefits to help them stand out from a cluttered marketplace, they execute their marketing to match their objectives.

**IMPACT** → *Clear Vision*

**BENEFITS** → *legit & long-lasting*

**OBJECTIVE** → *aspirational success*

**TARGET AUDIENCE** → *who you are talking to*

Your Clear Vision has an impact and benefits built into it already. It's your core concept and why it's important. Go back to your Aspirational Success to help identify the metrics, milestones, and intended results needed to achieve your Clear Vision at a high level of success. Your aspirational success is the objective of your Clear Vision.

**FIND YOUR CLEAR VISION**

Now you have the basics for how business branding translates into personal and professional branding. Let's look at how to position yourself in your career, business, or industry so you can shine.

Chapter 11

# POSITIONING
## What Makes You Visionary

**CLEAR VISION**
Clarify your future vision and what success looks like

**VISIONARY LEADER**
Express your clear vision through inspired action

*confidence*  *elevated expertise*

MONICA FELL IN LOVE AND HAD AN AFFAIR WITH HER boss when she was twenty-two. She has endured slut-shaming and cyberbullying on a global scale ever since. Know who I'm talking about?

Monica Lewinsky. It took her seventeen years to reinvent her story. In a 2014 essay with *Vanity Fair,* she declared it was time to "burn the beret and bury the blue dress" and

## POSITIONING

"bring a purpose to my past." She had been trying to reinvent herself for years with new jobs, a failed handbag line, even moving out of the US. The public wasn't ready for her, and you know why? She wasn't positioning herself in a way that would make an impression lasting longer than her past.

Here are the facts: she had an affair with a married man—some may say the most powerful man in the world at the time. Many so-called friends used the situation to their political benefit, and Monica was shamed and bullied for her actions for more than a decade. She desperately needed a reinvention and tried multiple times without any luck. It wasn't until she found her Clear Vision that she was able to push through her past, and she is now one of the most distinct and memorable voices against online bullying.

There are hundreds of ways to express yourself in your personal or professional brand using your voice and clear communication.

You know the power of words. Imagine you are listening to a riveting speech or watching that commercial that makes you tear up, or maybe you're at the concert of your dreams and your song comes on. At that moment, you let the words pour over you as your heart leaps out of your chest, tears well in your eyes, and your spirits rise beyond your physical body. You feel anything is possible as you listen with bated breath, ready to jump into action because their words are sewn with emotion and clarity. This is clear communication.

"Yes we can."

"Baby, you were born this way."

"Black Lives Matter."

"It's 5 o'clock somewhere."

People with a Clear Vision clearly communicate. How? By expanding their energy so much that it enables them to laser focus on words, ideas, and messages. They hold space for more ideas and insights because they've expanded the space between their thoughts to generate clarity.

The most powerful tool you have as a visionary is your voice. Your Inner Platform comes alive when your thoughts, feelings, and actions are aligned with your Outer Platform's expression. This is the goal of bringing who you are in your entirety to what you do. So let's look at how you can do that and not only manage your energy at a high level, but increase your expertise, authority, and influence to help create your Clear Vision.

## TARGET AUDIENCE

Your target audience is smaller than you think. It may even be one person.

Social media has us thinking we have to blanket the internet with our thoughts, feelings, and selfies, but to what end?

## POSITIONING

Circle back to what Aspirational Success looks like for you. What massive mindset shifts, micro and mini milestones are needed to achieve your Clear Vision at a high level of success? If you know where you are going, you'll know who you need to tell about it.

If you want to:

- Reinvent your career: share your vision with a targeted list of potential employers or somebody who knows somebody to get you in front of them.

- Increase your leadership role and your executive presence: share your vision with your boss and your team every day.

- Impact others or build your legacy: share your vision with those you want to impact and those who can help you do it.

- Become a sought-after speaker or expert in your field: share your vision with industry leaders and the individuals who book speakers.

- Build a business and create high-ticket clients: remind past clients that you are available and share with quality (not quantity) leads.

- Create a new income stream: share your vision with those you can serve and who need your product or service.

## FIND YOUR CLEAR VISION

When you narrow your field of focus it becomes very clear, very quickly, who you need to target to move your Clear Vision into reality. They call it a target audience for a reason, friend. Positioning yourself as a leader, legacy, or legend is up to you, and who you tell about it. The combination of your vision amplified with your voice and the right audience will position you as a visionary.

## 20/60/20 PRACTICE

Imagine that there are one hundred people who are following a certain social media account. Twenty of those people actively comment and like the content, because it speaks to them. They agree and it resonates with their values, which means they will share the account's posts and spread the good word because they believe in this account's social message. They are what I call "superfans."

Your superfans are your ride or die. And you, in turn, will ride or die for them. Superfans will follow you until the end of time because they believe in who you are and what you have to say. You inspire them, light them up, you may even be on their top ten list of people to have dinner with. These are your people, and this is who you are talking to.

I have a client who, in the height of the pandemic, searched Google for "A creative life purpose coach" and sure enough, my website popped up. Since then I have coached him, and over three dozen members of his executive strategic, creative, marketing, and operations teams. I've hosted multiple masterclasses and helped them envision multimillion-dollar ideas. He is my superfan, and I'm his.

Back to the social media account with one hundred followers. On the other end of the spectrum, there are twenty people who aren't in agreement with the message or intention of the account, and they'll let the account holder know. They are critical in the comments. They will share the content, but oftentimes in a hurtful or mocking way. They are resistant to the account's values and probably have social media accounts that share the exact opposite of what it stands for. These types of followers are called "crazy pants."

I have experience with crazy pants followers. There was a fake account created with a picture of me supposedly selling cryptocurrency. I've been called a fraud and been told my thinking is "galling" in the comments of an article I wrote for a very prominent design association. Did it hurt? Yes, but with massive forgiveness work and self-reflection I've come away stronger.

Your Paradox will have you spending time and energy trying to convince crazy pants followers that your pants somehow fit better than theirs with all the reasons why you are right, and they are wrong, or engaging with them to start a "healthy dialogue" which is a colossal waste of time and effort.

**FIND YOUR CLEAR VISION**

Instead, focus on the sixty people in the middle. These are the folks that see you and are listening, but they aren't quite ready to commit to you, or become a superfan. They know you and like you, but aren't sure if they are ready to buy from you or hire you. Know that they are out there, watching and reading what you share, and your voice is a gift. Keep going.

Share quick quips and snackable lessons through social media platforms like Instagram, TikTok, or LinkedIn. Or you can share in longer form content like writing your own blog, or articles for a publication. You could also be paid for your thought leadership through speaking opportunities, selling merchandise, or collaboration with other influencers and like-minded partnerships.

Your vision and voice are energy that spreads like wildfire. It is your role to generate the spark, to share from the warmth of knowing and standing in your bright flame of inspired action, knowing that your actions are in service of the superfans and the 60 percent who are there, listening.

Notice I haven't mentioned what the visual design of your brand looks like yet. And I'm a graphic designer! That's because what your personal or professional brand looks like is secondary to the confidence in who you are. You are the visionary, not the color, graphic, or visual appeal. Design elements will help tell the story—but, my friend, *you* are the story.

## POSITIONING: "WHAT DO I TALK ABOUT?"

### Create Your Authentic Voice and Message

**MINDSET**
Be in a relationship with your most vibrant self

→

**CREATIVITY**
Self-awareness, confidence, and executive presence

*self-awareness*

*authentic voice & message*

Someone told me that I have an "intuitive way" of being on social media. She said how I show up online is how I am in real life, that "both" of me were in alignment. I was thrilled! This way of being creates a sense of ease that I've been working towards for years.

My social media hasn't always been this way. I definitely struggled with what to share and what was "too much" and trying to impress others—all of which left me drained and attracting the wrong clients. Once I realized the "answer" to social media comes from a deep sense of knowing who I am and what lights me up, I was able to show up on social media freely without being attached to the results of likes, data, or insights, which ironically attracted my ideal clients.

Your fears, imposter syndrome, performance techniques, and Paradox will show up in your brand if you're not connected to your Inner Platform. They will bleed into your messaging as half-baked truths, semi-stands, and backseat bullies. You've seen this type of messaging; it's the individual that you have no connection to because they have no connection to themselves. They are wishy-washy in their messaging and inconsistent in how they show up, so, inevitably they become forgettable.

You're probably like, "That's great, Lisa, now what? How do I show up intuitively, and what the heck do I talk about?"

I get it. Imposter syndrome and my fear of standing out too much used to kick into high alert and would sometimes stop me mid-post, which is why I now rely on my Visionary Values to keep me moving forward with confidence on and offline.

Visionary Values will help anchor you into four high-level topics to always fall back on when you are sharing on or offline. When you begin to consistently implement conversations around these four ideas, then people will think of you when an opportunity arises because they'll think, "You know who always talks about pop culture? Danny! You should talk with them, let me introduce you."

Having four Visionary Values to shine out and share your vision with others will make it easy for them to see what you care about in a well-rounded way. They can see your north, south, east and west, and you can be both vulnerable and have boundaries when you set perimeters around what you share.

## POSITIONING

Visionary Values are built from your one-of-a-kind flavor of leadership. Let me explain.

I'm sure you've heard the conversation starter: "If you could have a dinner party with four people, dead or alive, who would they be?"

The Visionary Values brainstorming exercise kicks off with that idea in mind, but goes beyond the who and into the why. Why do you want to meet Wes Anderson? What about Drew Barrymore interests you? Why are you dying to know more about Shondaland?

We're going to look at why you chose these particular people to have a dinner party with and why you are attracted to them. To put it into branding terms—your dinner party invitees have a brand position, one that's attractive to you because you are their target audience. Their aspirational success and vision are aligned with something inside of you, so you look up to them for inspiration and motivation. Let's learn from them, peel back what they value, and reveal what Visionary Values you can aspire to and express in your Outer Platform.

## FIND YOUR VISIONARY VALUES

This can be done in one sitting if you are feeling inspired, or I have clients who take these questions with them over a week to explore, watch, and learn more about the people who inspire them.

**FIND YOUR CLEAR VISION**

## Part 1: Ask Yourself

Who lights me up?

Whom do I want to be in conversations with?

Who do I hang on their every word?

Is it an author or a poet? Maybe it's a celebrity. Maybe it's someone in your family, or maybe it is a politician. This can be somebody inside or outside of your industry.

It can be someone like Beyonce, RBG, Iris Apfel, Bruno Mars, Barack Obama, or that entrepreneur you love and double tap the like button every day on Instagram.

Generate a list of ten people who inspire you, alive or dead, real or fictional; it doesn't matter. It's your list of your top ten inspirational people.

## Part 2: Now, Write Down Why You Are Drawn to Them

What is it about this person that makes my heart sing?

What is their stand on life, politics, or culture that I love?

What about their approach to health or wellbeing am I enamored by?

## POSITIONING

What values do they embody in their personal and professional lives?

You are peeling back their Outer Platform—aka how they authentically share—to find what they value.

After you've generated a list, there are going to be underlying patterns in the values they hold as a group. Take a look at the qualities and similarities they share and try to narrow down the list to five similarities.

Mackenzie and I worked together at a very pivotal moment in her career when she upleveled from a project director to a principal consultant at a tech company. She has a very eclectic background, as her mother is white and her father is Indian. Growing up, she remembers not being able to quite place where she should be in the social structure of the United States, because she bounced between houses and lived in the US, China, and Germany.

Here's the list of who lit her up and why:

### Whitney Wolfe Herd

- The founder and CEO of Bumble, one of America's richest self-made women.

- Young, female and doesn't give a F.

- Kicks-ass and has a family life.

**FIND YOUR CLEAR VISION**

## *Ronda Jean Rousey*

- UFC and WWE mixed martial artist, judoka, and professional wrestler.

- First American woman to win an Olympic medal in judo in 2008.

- Focuses on body positivity.

## *Jacinda Ardern, The Prime Minister of New Zealand*

- World's youngest female head of government at age thirty-seven.

- Attended the United Nations general assembly meeting with a three-month-old baby.

- Exemplifies grace under fire, particularly during the pandemic.

## *Lizzo*

- Grammy Award winning singer, rapper, and songwriter.

- Advocate for body positivity, self-love, sexuality, and Black pride.

- She plays a mean flute and can throw down R&B with the best of them.

### *Barack and Michelle Obama*

- First black presidential family.

- Calm, cool, collected, very relatable.

- Withstood a lot of racism which takes inner strength and conviction.

### *Megan Rose Lane*

- A twenty-something London-based beauty blogger and podcaster focused on motherhood, mental health, and confidence.

- Not afraid to show the real and unedited side of social media.

- Has a mixed-race daughter.

As we went through the list, we noticed that many of the people she was inspired by are trailblazers; they were the first person to carve out a path that didn't exist before.

## FIND YOUR CLEAR VISION

Whitney Wolfe Herd successfully founded a multi-billion-dollar company.

Ronda Jean Rousey was the first female ultimate fighting champion.

There was no one ahead of them to look up to, yet here they are, showing up because they believed in themselves, their values, and, as a result, they've become an inspiration to others.

We also noticed that some of the people she shared, like Lizzo and Megan Rose, are proactively body positive. They shine a bright light on showing up as themselves, even if it doesn't match what mainstream media has deemed traditionally sexy or beautiful. They don't take shit from anyone, and their confidence shines through their words and actions.

Mackenzie's boss passed away from COVID in the early months of the pandemic. She didn't have a mentor to show her how to lead her team. She was thrown into the fire of a high-tech firm and asked to fight fire with everything she had. She, like the people she is inspired by, is a kick-ass fighter.

We also noticed that her list was a mix of different races and cultural backgrounds, like Lizzo and Megan Rose, and many of them value their family life, like Jacinda and the Obamas. Mackenzie's Indian background has her surrounded by family and, like them, she is very family oriented.

## POSITIONING

Having people whom she can see as both professional and fully themselves in their skin is inspirational. She loved how the Obama administration showed the public how Sasha and Malia were growing up, two young pre-teen to teenage girls raised in the spotlight, with grace and a sense of normalcy, even under fire from the various news outlets. Family life, and seeing how to weave it into professional life with grace, is important to Mackenzie.

Visionary Values: Fighter, grace, family, body positive, trailblazer.

As I reflected the list of qualities back to Mackenzie, she said, "Of course, I believe in those things, doesn't everyone?"

The simple answer is no. Not at all. These values were unique to her. After seeing her values in a different and brighter light, she updated her LinkedIn headline to read:

> **PRINCIPAL CONSULTANT | TRAILBLAZER**
> I am a trailblazing leader packed with empathy, using my unique combination of grit and grace to inspire people to be their best selves, in order to do their best work.

Look at your list of people, begin to circle or highlight the qualities, values, and patterns you see. Maybe it's the role they are

## FIND YOUR CLEAR VISION

in, maybe they are all athletes, creatives, or parents. Maybe some of them are advocates for gun control or mid-century modern art collecting. Maybe they are celebrities who care about the environment.

Are they Broadway actors, even though you can't sing or dance worth a dime? No problem. The underlying patterns, values, and ideas that you see are a list of the highest qualities you admire in others. Broadway actors are outgoing, tenacious, bold; they're probably fit and very aware of how to use their bodies to evoke emotions.

Your list of people embodies a certain flavor of leadership that is important to you. Your list is motivational and inspirational to you, not anyone else—these are your people. This is what makes it personal, and guess what—those same values you appreciate in others are also your values.

I'm not big on professional assessments. They will tell you that who you are is like 33 percent of the rest of the population. Your Visionary Values can't be found in an assessment, because this is you. These are the intuitive, magnetic values that light you up and can lead your personal or professional brand positioning, what topics you talk about—hell, even what you put in your LinkedIn headline.

You may think it's no big deal to see what you highly value and are inspired by written out plainly in front of you—because your soul already knew they were within you to begin with. Now you are present to who you can become,

## POSITIONING

and these values will become the flavor of your leadership and brand messaging.

Download the Visionary Values worksheet at:
www.bebrightlisa.com/findyourclearvision-book

## FIND YOUR VOICE

Certain designers and artists become visionary because people are drawn to their style and artistic voice.

Think of the Japanese artist Yayoi Kusama, who painted red and white polka dots to make sense of her mental illness and hallucinations. She said, "I fight pain, anxiety, and fear every day, and the only method I have found that relieves my illness is to keep creating art. I followed the thread of art and somehow discovered a path that would allow me to live."

Think of Kehinde Wiley, who painted Barack Obama's official presidential portrait. At the time, there were forty-three other portraits of past presidents, but Kehinde's voice, style, and creative expression embody his flavor of creativity seen through the lens of a modern Black artist. Kehinde reminds us that "we all look at the same object in different ways."

Think of Zaha Hadid, who became the first female to win the Pritzker Prize, architecture's most coveted award. "I used to not like being called a 'woman architect.' I'm an architect, not just a woman architect. The guys used to tap me on the head and say, 'You're okay for a girl.' But I see an incredible amount of need from other women for reassurance that it can be done, so I don't mind anymore."

Artists share their deepest ideas through paint, color, and texture, expressing their voice through visuals, which leaves us, the viewer, with a sense of what they are feeling. Great art leaves a lasting impression. What you share through your Visionary Values can be expressed in the same way artists do, into the topics or concepts you resonate with, and how you share it becomes your medium.

As Mackenzie and I continued to look at her Visionary Values, other concepts began to arise. Most of the people she was inspired by are financially well-off, and she loves to talk about money. She spends her free time reading up on financial ideologies like F.I.R.E. (Financial Independence, Retire Early) and how to invest money.

Some people find talking about money taboo, but Mackenzie can talk about money for hours. The topic of money naturally attracts or repels people, which also means it can be a distinct and memorable connection moment between her and her audience.

## What Can You Talk about for Hours?

Someone who has zero interests or hobbies, and is frankly bored with who they are in their life, is as intriguing as a doorknob. What can you talk about until the wee hours of the morning?

## What Lights You Up?

You are the popping reinvention of your former self who's filled with excitement—someone who, through this work, knows what topics, ideas, concepts, and ways of being light you up. Get excited!

Sharing, showing up, and being in conversations doesn't mean you have to know everything about a topic. The world doesn't need more experts; we need more energy. You don't have to have traveled to the moon to talk about your fascination with moon cycles or "Ancient Aliens" on *The History Channel*. You don't have to be in a political office to be an activist. You simply have to bring energy with you into the conversation, the post, or the presentation and then take inspired action.

## What's Yours to Own That Is No One Else's?

Think about your cultural and racial background. No one had your parents or your childhood, and absolutely no one lives in your skin—you are you for a reason. Share who you are with pride.

Growing up with divorced parents, Mackenzie felt that when she was with her Indian father, she had to blend in with his new family, and vice versa when she stayed with her mother. Two different religions, two cultures, and two levels of parental expectations had her thinking that being bi-racial meant she was not a whole person; instead, she was two halves of a whole—this, or that—which left her feeling torn, separate, and alone.

After seeing her Visionary Values, she received a creative download and shifted from an either/or mindset to a both/and, which instantly bloomed into stories that blended together who she was because of her unique experience of being raised in both an Indian and a white American household. She began to weave both/and into her love for cooking chocolate sweets—the blend of turmeric and lavender, or sea salt and cardamom chocolates. Sounds deliciously divine, right?

## What in Your Background Can You Own, Express, and Share?

No one else has experienced life like you.

Think of your Visionary Values as they relate to your gender or sexual identity.

Have you not fully expressed yourself because you don't know where you land in the heteronormative social structure? Well, cool! This is your opportunity to stand up and shine your bright light, my friend, because who you are is a gift. Your experience as a human on this earth, at this time, is a gift to share with

## POSITIONING

us. Your energy, your presence, and your stories are what are yours to share. Define them using the Visionary Values framework, and you will never be short on what to talk about.

You are a prism of both/and, not either/or. You are the trailblazer of you.

## EVERYTHING'S COMING UP A.C.E.S. (AUTHORITY, CONNECT, ENGAGE, SHINE)

**EXPANDED ENERGY**
Rituals and habits to expand personal energy

*inspirational*

→

**CLEAR COMMUNICATION**
Model transformational leadership through messaging, motivation and transparency

*transformational leader*

Visionary Values help you brainstorm what to talk about. Now, we need to know how to talk about it. The A.C.E.S. framework for clear communication gives you a bird's-eye view of how to share your message with your audience. It will make you both relatable and an authority, simply because you are consistent and organized in what you share.

This framework can be used to create content for social media. It also comes into play when connecting with people for a new position, or when you have just joined a new team.

Whether you use it in a formal structure, like in your social media content, or informally as a connection moment at those awkward networking events, it's a tool to have in your back pocket to help shine a light on what you care about so others can connect with you.

## Authority: Have a Point of View and Stick to It

People are buying from other businesses and hiring other people. You can no longer be the best-kept secret; you have to share your expertise with executive presence and personal leadership. Plus, sharing your expertise is sharing your truth—if it's true, it's not bragging. It's a gift to share with others who need your knowledge.

I hosted a five-day masterclass about the Inner Platform, and on day three I pulled what I thought was a Tarot card, to share with the attendees. It turns out I was pulling from an Oracle deck. A couple of days later, I was following up with an attendee who was a marketing executive and reiki master. She told me the difference between Oracle cards and Tarot cards. Tarot card decks typically have seventy-eight cards and are based on the traditional Rider-Waite deck. Oracle cards can have any number of different cards in their deck and are based on a theme like intuition or energy.

This wasn't the point of our conversation. We were actually talking about how she didn't know what she was an expert in because she was so multi-passionate. I paused her right then and there. "Do you realize you just corrected me, a novice, with expert advice?" She didn't; she thought she was just helping me out. No! Not at all! She was kind in correcting me with authority. She didn't realize that she was more of an authority than I was until I reflected it back to her.

Be the expert you already are. Share with joy, because people want to know what you know. What can you teach or lead others about? What idea or insight can you share?

If you don't know, ask. Other people can see your essence and expertise a lot more easily than you can.

- Take a stand and share your viewpoint. Think of Megan Markle, the Duchess of Sussex, and her podcast, Archetypes, where she dissects the labels that try to hold women back.

- Lead uncomfortable conversations. Think Emmanuel Acho and his breakthrough video series and book, *Uncomfortable Conversations with a Black Man*.

- Create research opportunities and share your progress. Think of my friend Andy Crestodina, co-founder of Orbit Media, sharing blogging research since 2014.

- Give compassionate advice. Think Byron Katie and "The Work," or Brené Brown leading conversations about shame and vulnerability, or any leading life and leadership coach who gives compassionate advice.

You don't have to have written a book, or have your website polished and perfected with published articles in *Forbes* or *Huffington Post;* you simply need to be two or three chapters ahead of your audience. They need to know how to get to the next step in their journey with you as their guide.

Your personal or professional voice is created one word and one share at a time, consistently. Stay connected to your Clear Vision and expanded energy, and your voice will flow.

Write down two to three areas that you are an expert in and declare yourself an authority starting today.

## Connect: Connect through Personal Stories

People relate to visionaries because they feel connected to them, because they've seen a side of them that makes them human, and they think, "That person has the same problems I do! They can't get their kids out the door either!" Or, "They had the same job as me when they started out, and now look at them."

A moment of connection isn't groundbreaking or prolific. It can be done in a handshake, hug, or even a tender smile. It's showing up with your humanity in full view and being relatable. Underneath the "stuff," we're all human.

## POSITIONING

My friend Marti Konstant is a career coach, *Forbes* contributor, global speaker, and authority in workplace agility. She wrote the book *Activate Your Agile Career*. In one of her recent LinkedIn posts, she shared photos of her at-home workspace, which she had updated with a green screen, a circle light, and a standing desk. She gave us a behind-the-scenes look at her life—which stood out against what I typically see on LinkedIn. I clicked through the photos in the carousel and took note of her setup and webcam. It was really useful. It wasn't her typical type of LinkedIn post. Instead, it was personal and immediately connected me to her in a deeper way.

This is an example of how to connect through personal stories. People want to see you being yourself.

Here are a few sentence stems to get your energy flowing towards purposeful connection:

"I used to _____. Now I _____."

- I used to go to bed at midnight, now I get eight hours of sleep, and it's done miracles to my energy and focus.

- I used to think I had to work my ass off in order to advance my career; now I realize the best leaders have the best self-care, and I log off completely every weekend.

## FIND YOUR CLEAR VISION

- I used to give all of my energy and attention to my kids; now I've hired support to create a better morning routine before school drop-off for all of us.

Identify two to three stories from your past that you can share to connect with others or something you can share from "behind-the-scenes" that will create a moment of connection.

### Engage: Be Someone You'd Want to Have a Conversation with

After a moment of connection, the next level is to engage through active listening.

Active listening is a key trait for visionaries. This is your ability to focus on what the other person is saying and to listen in between the lines of what is being said and not said. In the coaching world, we call this "holding space." I read non-fiction books with a highlighter, highlighting the key concepts of a chapter so I can go back in the future and quickly grasp the essence of the idea. Imagine that active listening is like highlighting the essence of a conversation and reflecting it back in real time so the speaker feels seen and heard.

People seek validation for their ideas. It's a function of our Ego and pride reflecting back that we "get you" in a deep way so you feel welcome in our space. Be compassionate, curious, open, and willing to have a real conversation. A core competency of being a professional coach is to actively listen so we can hold space and reflect language back to our clients, and though it doesn't sound very intuitive, we often memorize a series of questions and prompts to dig deeper and lead our clients through the conversation.

Get curious with people you want to engage with by asking probing questions that touch on their humanity.

"Tell me more about…"

"And then what happened?"

"How did that make you feel?"

"What about you?"

"What did you learn?"

"What are you going to do next?"

People don't follow people who only talk about themselves and to themselves with no doorway open to engage, because it's no fun to be in a one-way narcissistic relationship. Am I right?

Memorize a series of questions, or at least have one or two in your back pocket so you'll be ready when someone wants to engage with you and share from their heart. You can engage on social media as well by participating in the comments of people you are interested in on Instagram or LinkedIn, for example. A thoughtful comment on a post speaks volumes; it signals to the author that you found their content valuable enough to read and engage with.

Take it a step further by popping into their DMs and saying something about how you appreciated their post. This is a great way to move from talking to everyone into a private conversation.

To engage with your audience, practice active listening and holding space. Prompt further conversation by asking questions.

## Shine Bright: Let Your Quirkiness Shine

Your Visionary Values are the diamonds that help you shine bright. They are the gems that you could talk about for hours, the topics and ideas that you nerd out on when you are alone or with your closest friends.

Maybe documentary films about the ocean make you drool with excitement, or the New York graffiti scene makes you giddy every time a train passes. You may think to yourself, "Why in the world would anybody care to talk to me about graffiti?"

Guess what? I used to hang out with graffiti kids in San Francisco when I was in art school in the '90s. We'd take dozens

## POSITIONING

of stickers from the post office, and write our tags on them with sharpie markers and walk around the city for hours at night. Mature? No. Professional? No, but it's endlessly fun to talk about now.

Your quirky pop-culture, indie obsession is a conversation starter. It's you. It lights you up and gives you energy. It's a bright, shiny, popping moment.

My client, Lily, is a tutor for middle-school students in Chicago. She's an authority of knowledge and has an eagerness to learn, leaving her client roster fully booked. You wouldn't hire a tutor for your 8th grader if that tutor wasn't excited about history, mathematics, or social studies.

Lily also loves medieval Viking history, and it's become a hobby for her. She reads books about voyages in her spare time, watches all of the *History Channel* specials, and can talk about Viking lore for days. She loves it, and so do other people!

Another client is a Creative Director at a multimedia entertainment company in Hollywood. He loves Serena and Venus Williams and Mary-Kate and Ashely Olsen; both duos are highly ambitious, powerful sisters. Get him talking about their rise to stardom, and he can go on for hours. It's endlessly entertaining and insightful!

People hire people they can relate to, or when they see the value in what they do and the energy they get from doing their work.

## FIND YOUR CLEAR VISION

**What kinky, quirky, fun-loving thing do you love to do in your spare time? How can you shine?**

My clients shine bright because they are a:

Nike Sneaker-head-loving FAIA architect

Amish butchery-loving project delivery director

Jurassic Park-loving SVP of strategy

NFL-loving master life coach

CrossFit-loving therapist

LGBTQI+ community-loving EVP of creative

Dog rescue-loving art director

It's your story, your life, and yes, your audience wants to know. Sharing will manifest in ideal opportunities, career advancement, and influence. Stories that are unique to you can include your ethnicity, identity, and race. Or your musical interest and fashion sense. Your passion and dreams. Your daydreams and nightmares. Your disdain and your love. Shine your quirkiness with pride.

Resurrect stories from your past that you learned a lesson from, something that was small or big and exciting. Gems are found in the small and big moments. Brainstorm ideas, starting with the sentence stem, "Two things you don't know about me are…"

The best stories are the ones that stick and are retold, sometimes embellished, and are made to be memorable.

## STORYTELLING: PEOPLE WANT TO KNOW YOU

Storytelling is what makes a personal brand personal. It's why we read books and watch television series until the finale. We want to be entertained, learn, and make meaning in our lives.

I can't tell you how often I hear my mentor, Brendon Burchard, say, "I'm just a boy from Montana." Or he says, "In Montana, we always say you need a map before you go into the woods." He is using language and a place to relate to people like me, just a girl from Missouri.

The relatability and consistency make him feel like he's the guy down the street from Montana, so people like me start to know, like, and trust him. Never mind that he's a multi-millionaire icon in the personal development and influencer marketing community with over one million followers on Instagram alone, who lives part-time on the beach in Puerto Rico.

Telling stories about yourself is vulnerable by nature and may not be something that comes naturally, so it's worthwhile to start small and practice. Brainstorm a few stories to share and take notice of what stories you are always telling your clients, friends, or colleagues. Sharing from a place that is true to you, and, more importantly, to who you are becoming will show that you are a trustworthy and relatable human being.

Write down two to three stories that you find yourself telling again and again. Brainstorm a few quips that you say that other people find funny or interesting. People find it endearing that I grew up in Missouri and moved as far away as I could when I turned 18, to San Francisco. Now I'm just trying to find a way back to the lake I grew up on in Missouri.

Your personal brand needs to be a consistent experience across multiple social channels and a personal brand website. Think of your bio on Instagram, your About section on LinkedIn, and your website. These are all places people are reading about you and receiving the emotional connection you intend to create. Make it consistent, impactful, and memorable.

## THE ABOUT ME PAGE COCKTAIL

The "About Me" page is the most visited web page on business and personal brand websites because people hire people. Your audience wants to know how you can help them solve their "problem."

People are looking for ways to solve their problems, and they happened upon you because they hope you are their solution. Think about it. This is why people type questions into Google's search bar. Instead of typing in "personal brand designer,"

## POSITIONING

they would type, "Someone to help me build my personal brand." Now you simply have to align your expertise to their problem, and boom. You are the solution to their problem.

Sometimes we have trouble sharing our accomplishments and expertise, but this, my friend, is not the time to downplay who you are and what you believe. Nobody wants a weak pour.

The About Me Page Cocktail is a framework to generate the content to use on your About Page, whether that is on your website, LinkedIn, or the details of a cover letter.

The About Me Cocktail is a delicious blend of why your people should reach out and work, hire, or partner with you. Not everyone is a match for you—just think about mixing a cocktail with too many ingredients. It tastes awful and gives you a headache, so let's keep it simple by following this recipe.

My friend, Colleen Arturi, a personal brand storyteller, shared in a post:

When it comes to you and your story, stop trying to sell people on your achievements alone.

People will not remember how much you raised the numbers.

They will remember how you treated them while boosting those numbers.

## FIND YOUR CLEAR VISION

People will not remember how many units were sold last year.

They will remember how good it felt to celebrate with you at the end-of-year party.

People will not remember what your master's degree is in.

People will remember how it felt to be in a room with you.

Focus on defining how you show up for others, and the rest will fall into place.

## FOUR PARTS ABOUT YOU

### 1. Share Your Mission

To share the beginning of your Clear Vision, use the sentence stem: "I help (your audience) (create this result), and this is important because…."

Pick your poison, the thing you do to create the action of your vision:

I help

I create

I give

## POSITIONING

I teach

I empower

I like to say, "I help my clients find their Clear Vision."

My client, Dominic, is the VP Creative Director at a global entertainment network. He says, "I unlock a brand's value through storytelling."

My client, Brianna, is a lawyer in D.C. She says, "I'm an employment lawyer on a mission to empower other millennial leaders."

This one-liner is great to use in your headline on LinkedIn.

## 2. Backstory

What got you to where you are today? There are stories from your past that led you to create your vision. Brainstorm the top three professional or personal moments that led you here. What are you known for doing? List three things. Brainstorm the big and little things. You can edit them later. This is where you can brag, and it's not time to humblebrag. Brag, seriously. We are sharing what's true.

As a professional you've had prior success. People will naturally believe that you have authority as a professional in your new career or business as well.

## FIND YOUR CLEAR VISION

## 3. Your Personal or Professional Evolution

This is where you can showcase how you have changed, adapted, or grown into the person you are now. Your evolution story makes you human. Consider using the sentence stem we started in the A.C.E.S. framework: "I used to _____. Now I _____."

What life advice do clients always come to you for? And what do you say?

Remember my client Gwyn from Chapter 6? She used to micromanage and double-check everyone's work. Now she is curious, visionary, and trusts herself.

It's human to show a side of you that wasn't perfect but has evolved into a person who is relatable and growing.

## 4. Your "Ah-ha!" Moment

What moment, event, or thing helped you end up right where you are now? The Ah-ha moment typically comes at the bottom of a breakdown. It's an insight or event that "changed everything" or at least something that made you want to share yourself in a bigger way.

Think of the event that prompted you to get a drastic haircut, thinking, "This will change everything!"

**POSITIONING**

What was that thing that had you break down? People want to hear about it. It makes you relatable and their lives seem doable. If you can get through it and be who you are, sharing with heart and having survived, they can learn from you.

Brianna, the D.C. lawyer, shares on her website, "I spent years contorting myself into the shape of what I had been taught a 'good lawyer' should be before I came to recognize that my professional achievements were out of step with what I knew to be most important to me."

## FOUR PARTS ABOUT THEM

### 1. Who Are You Talking To?

Who are the people you serve and why are they looking you up online? Simply put, this is your target audience. Let them know you see them and that they are in the right place by calling them out directly:

"You're an editor looking for…"

"Many black professionals…"

"You're a homeowner ready to…"

Dominic says, "Many brands in entertainment haven't reached their full potential in value…"

## 2. What Are You Offering Them?

Clearly explain what you are offering your audience so they know what they get when they work, hire, or partner with you. This is a list of your services but written in sentence format (yep, you are going to be repetitive. It's okay, people love reminders and need the repetition to make it stick).

Dominic says, "So what I do is build brands to extend the cultural importance and create fandom. My process results in shape-shifting relevance and driving storytelling through loyal fans."

## 3. Testimonial

You can't say how cool you are, but other people can! In the middle of client engagements, and at the end of our time together, I ask my clients to fill out a Google Form with their feedback on their experience working with me. At the end of the form, I ask if I can use their feedback as a testimonial and if they'd like to remain anonymous. It's a nice way to turn the tables and ask the client to be the expert on why they chose to work together in the first place.

Ask someone what it was like before you started working together, and what changed for them after.

You may have a feeling of "Gosh, it would be awkward to ask someone for personal feedback about me." Get over it—you

## POSITIONING

are playing the game of attracting high vibrational energy, not repelling it. By not telling your story, using your voice, and creating moments of trust, you are lowering your energetic exchange. Do it.

### 4. Your C.T.A. = Call to Action

People want to know what to do next. They've found you. Now you need to tell them what the next step is: how to book you to speak, how to get in touch, how to work with you, how to hire you. Give them a clear call to action so they know how to take the next step so you can help them solve their problem.

On Brianna's contact page, she says, "Book me to write or speak, or set up a time to chat using this form."

Download the About Me Page Cocktail worksheet at www.bebrightlisa.com/findyourclearvision-book

> **BRIGHT TOOL: OUTER PLATFORM CHECK-IN**
>
> - Your voice expresses itself in the choices you make. Make sure the companies and philanthropic work you do aligns with your future vision.
>
> - Your voice is your brand. Be consistent through clear communication.

## FIND YOUR CLEAR VISION

- Take ownership of your feelings—aim to get to Neutral, then go up from there.

- Double-check your intentions before speaking. Is it your Paradox or your most vibrant self leading the conversation?

- Be personal and present—there is nothing worse than being led by someone who is being led by their phone. Make eye contact and be in the moment now.

- Don't make others right and wrong—it's not your business. You are here to rally the 20 percent who already believe in your vision and the 60 percent who are quietly waiting to hear more from you.

Practice doesn't make perfect, but it makes progress. Keep showing up and sharing. Practice sharing who you are from a high level of intention and energy, and I promise you: opportunities will arise that are aligned with your Clear Vision. When people see your Clear Vision expressed, then you become visionary.

Chapter 12

# MESSAGING AND VISUAL CONTENT
## Branding Is Moot If You Can't Master Your Mindset

**INNER TRUST**
Trust yourself and
your decisions

*resilient*

**TRUSTWORTHY**
Active listening, adaptability and
integrity creates genuine connection

*career advancement*

"What's catfishing, mommy?" my daughter asked.

I grew up on a lake in Missouri with catfishes in it, but still felt unsure of my answer. "It's not fishing for catfish?"

"I don't think so," she replied; "it was a man on TV who wore a wig to fool his friends."

## MESSAGING AND VISUAL CONTENT

When I see a new phrase on social media, I go to my trusted source: UrbanDictionary.com.

Catfishing: "The phenomenon of internet predators that hide who they really are by fabricating online identities to hook people into emotional/romantic relationships online."

It's no wonder we have issues trusting people. We are protecting ourselves, our hearts, and our reputation from cruel deception.

When sharing your personal or professional brand, you ideally want to create a space where people feel safe to be with you and your vision, where they can trust that you are who you say you are.

Maybe you're thinking, "But, Lisa, is anyone going to care what I have to say?" That isn't the right question. This is your Paradox wanting to be validated and liked. The real question is "How can I be trustworthy so people feel safe and connected to me?"

Branding designers and advertising agencies design icons, symbols, graphics, and messages that, when put together repeatedly, create an emotional response, and over time the hope is that you will get to know them, like them, and trust them.

"Know, Like, Trust" is a bedrock marketing theory that easily translates from big marketing budgets into personal branding.

## FIND YOUR CLEAR VISION

Think of someone you admire in the media, like an actor. If they promote a certain skincare line, or a book, you probably buy it. I know that when I'm done reading a fiction book, I head to Reese Witherspoon's book club on Instagram to find my next juicy read.

Reese Witherspoon is someone I trust to have a book recommendation that's right up my alley. And here's why: she's built her personal brand over time, allowing me to get to know her outside of her acting career through her media company, *Hello Sunshine*, which focuses exclusively on stories for and about women.

When I was in Nashville a few years ago, I had to pop into her store, Draper James. When I walked into the shop, I was handed a lemonade in a navy blue cup with a striped paper straw. Very on-brand with her southern charm. And although I'm not a preppy dresser, I did find a denim maxi dress, which I bought so I could say I bought something at Reese Witherspoon's store.

Reese Witherspoon's personal brand is carefully thought out and executed, so let's take a look at how to create this type of consistent brand experience for you. Branding designers choose photography, colors, typography, and symbols that, if the business says what it means and means what it says, represent that you can trust them.

I got to "know" Reese from her movies like *Cruel Intentions*, *Election*, and *Sweet Home Alabama*. I started to like her—outside of the characters she plays—when I saw her in person at a *Hello Sunshine* event with Glennon Doyle, Abby Wambach, and Luvvie Ajayi Jones, among others. After bringing together such a cool in-person event with diversity and purpose, I started to trust her. Now I buy the books she recommends and maxi dresses because I know, like, and trust her.

To bring your Clear Vision to life, we want others to know us, like us, and trust us too. Not everyone will, and that's okay. It's okay not to be liked by everyone. We simply want to connect with the 20 percent who already love us and can help spread the word.

## LET OTHER PEOPLE GET TO KNOW YOU

The visual design of a brand is meant to make you feel a certain way when you look at it or experience it. It's in essence playing with your emotions. When I was inside Draper James, light country music was playing in the background, a candle smelled of just mowed grass, I was surrounded by charming blue and white gingham shirts, button-downs, puffy bows, and wainscoting.

Is that whole southern charm thing for everyone? No, but it spoke to me, and I readily bought it.

Here's an easy example of how branding makes you feel. Let's try on shoes.

## FIND YOUR CLEAR VISION

Think of a Nike commercial. The twenty-something athlete is outside in the rain, taking their last lap around the track, unwilling to stop even though it's pouring. They just do it, people!

Now think of a Skechers commercial. A forty-something B-list celebrity, like Tony Romo or Brooke Burke, is walking through an outdoor mall feeling super bouncy and having a good time because their feet feel amazing in the extra soft Skechers shoes they are rocking with their comfy white ankle socks.

Both companies sell shoes for active people, but you feel the difference in the emotional realm they are playing in, which is going to attract different customers.

Human beings do the same thing. We attract people based on the feeling we give them, and depending on how you look at it, we can catfish people with falsehoods or embrace them with authenticity and transparency. The same goes for inspiring outer trust. The only way to inspire outer trust is to shine it out from the inside—be a role model of your flavor of leadership and Visionary Values.

Trust is seen and felt in expressive qualities. I may trust someone who is colorful, bold, and daring, and you may trust someone who is calm, introspective, and reflective. What type of shoe experience do you gravitate towards: Nike, Skechers, or high heels? Maybe Crocs, or better yet, Crocs with socks?

**MESSAGING AND VISUAL CONTENT**

# WHAT'S YOUR BRAND GOING TO LOOK LIKE?

## Visual Branding and Presence

A picture, or a great outfit, speaks a thousand words. Your visual presence arrives when you enter a real room or an online one. It's your demeanor, your attitude, energy, and outfit. It's your visual communication, from the colors you choose to wear to the typography and messaging on your social channels. People need constant reminders that you are you—maybe even one thousand reminders, so creating the verbal and visual content of your personal and professional brand is time well spent.

Clear communication is something visionary people practice through words and visual presence.

President Biden was sworn into office on a bitingly cold January morning. It wasn't his acceptance speech that was memorable, or Lady Gaga's bulletproof dress with the extra-large dove of peace, though it was gorgeous.

It was Amanda Gorman. Her bright yellow jacket and red headband on top of her braids felt like a glowing sunrise on a cold land. Amanda, who was twenty-three years old when she read her poem, "The Hill We Climb," left the country in an afterglow of hope and inspiration for a better future, a place to look forward to.

Amanda may not have considered herself a visionary for a new generation of poets or people craving hope, creativity, and inspiration during a dark time in history, but she has stepped into the role with grace and intention.

Amanda's visual presence embodies her personal brand. Her red headband was an intentional choice: "I highly suggest a headband crown for anyone wanting to stand taller, straighter, and prouder."

Her words, purposeful and practiced, are her medium. Amanda grew up with a speech impediment, to which she said, "The only thing that can impede me is myself."

Since that bright day, big brands have wanted to partner with Amanda to cascade her memorable glow on their products. She turned down a record $17M in promotional opportunities before agreeing to become Estée Lauder's Global Changemaker. Her vision wasn't to be another "face" of a cosmetic company. Instead, she has used her personal brand to align with a company that will partner with her to bring change to the beauty industry for people of color, and bring much-needed money (like $3M worth) to promote literacy among women and girls.

Amanda's gift as a poet lit up the world. Her presence is stuck in our memory forever. She showed the world who she is, and her beliefs, and has since partnered with brands she aligns with, and written many award-winning books.

Let's break down how to move from your Clear Vision into messaging, and build a visual presence through branding techniques.

**MESSAGING AND VISUAL CONTENT**

There are six brand elements when it comes to building a business, personal, or professional brand. It's not rocket science. Sure, you can pay top dollar for advertising and marketing agencies, but at the heart of it, these six elements can consistently carry your vision forward so your presence is memorable and people can get to know you, like you, and trust you.

## PERSONAL OR PROFESSIONAL BRAND STYLE GUIDE

1. Tone of Voice

2. Your Name

3. Color

4. Typography

5. Photography

6. Gimmick Limit

Download your brand style guide at www.bebrightlisa.com/findyourclearvision-book

### Tone of Voice

The words you choose and your tone of voice leave a lasting impression. Sometimes they create magic and connection, sometimes heartbreak and confusion. We know this to be true because what you say sticks. Words have a magnetism that attracts or repels people. Share from your Clear Vision, and you become a visionary. Share from your Paradox, you get more of the same. Your tone of voice is your personality shining through your word choice and the message you are sending.

Consider your tone of voice an extension of your personality and expertise. The VP of strategy for a multi-media company will have a different tone of voice than a fitness instructor. Put thought into your word choice and how you choose to say it. It will leave an impression.

**Your Name**

In business branding, this would be your logo, but for personal or professional branding, you don't necessarily need a nice tidy logo that may feel too contrived. Instead, think about how you can creatively use your name. My client's name is Barbara Best, and she signs her emails, "Best always, Barbara."

I took my husband's last name when we were married, and it's been tricky. People often get embarrassed because they don't know how to pronounce Guillot, so they'll skip over it in an introduction. In my signature at the bottom of my emails, I phonetically spell it out so it helps people remember. Lisa Guillot (Ghee-O). When I send it to someone who is interviewing me on a podcast, I'll add a second reference, (Guillot, like Guillotine without the T). This helps ease the embarrassment of not knowing or having to ask.

My Aunt Kay became Dr. Andreoli and built a professional name for herself as the Dean of nursing at Rush University in Chicago in the '90s. When she divorced, she didn't want to keep her ex-husband's last name but decided for professional reasons to do so. Changing your last name is something to consider as you are building your reputation over time.

## Color

Color is my favorite element of branding. Bright, beautiful, and bold color is my jam. Literally think of raspberry jam with a side of orange marmalade. Yours may be more subdued, preppy, traditional, or eccentric. Color choice weaves into your fashion choices, and wearing certain colors can enhance your natural skin tone, making you look effortlessly beautiful. Color is also a way to create attention in a cluttered online world. Being consistent will make the biggest difference.

An easy way to find your color as it relates to personal branding is to look in your closet to see what color of clothes is most represented. Is your closet filled with warm jewel tones like you see in fall or the cool blues and greens of springtime? What two or three colors show up most often in your wardrobe? What color do people always say, "Damn, Queen, you look amazing! That is your color—you should wear it more often!!"

## FIND YOUR CLEAR VISION

Color is compartmentalized into the four seasons.

**Winter:** think of light starting to peek through after a snowstorm: creamy whites, grays, and the tan of the landscape. Or on an ice-cold clear day mixed with midnight blue, a deep rich red, and a neutral like stone or tan. Avoid red and green combinations as it's an instant reminder of Christmas.

Think Angelina Jolie.

**Spring:** light, warm pops of color like grass green, canary yellow, and peaches. Avoid pairing too many pastels because it teeters on childish. But a lush lavender looks great paired with mustard yellow.

Think Gayle King.

**Summer:** lighten up with ocean blues, bright sunny yellows, and watermelon pink; these are like spring but bolder and hotter. Neon may be over the top, but a vibrant green or lemon juice yellow will make you stand out. Pair it with a black, and you've made a statement.

Think Iris Apfel.

**Fall:** deep, warm jewel tones like burnt orange, ruby red, violet, and warm browns. Think of the leaves changing in the Midwest, or of a handful of gemstones like rubies, emeralds, and amethysts.

Think Ralph Lauren.

**Neutral Classic:** think Adele with her high glam makeup of creams, peaches, and a black cat-eye. A neutral palette is always a classic; just make sure it has crisp details and is tailored. It's Adele, not Gap khakis circa 1990.

**Black and white** are an easy color combination—I suggest throwing in one more color to mix it up and add your special splash of personality. Red, for example, is an instant classic. But, what tone of red? Vampire red, blood red, valentine red, pink-red, orange-red, or stop sign red? I could go on and on.

Color creates emotion; that's why artists go through their "blue period." That's why there are so many shades of eyeshadow at MAC Cosmetics. Search for color trends online and find something that sticks with you and your personality and start to "try it on" in your wardrobe and your personal marketing.

## Typography

Your font choice makes your words come alive. Think of typing something in a lowercase versus an uppercase bold italic.

hello.

***HELLO!***

## FIND YOUR CLEAR VISION

Typography, which is the art of arranging letters for print, speaks in different ways. Typography styles come in two forms: serif and sans serif.

Serif fonts have the little feet on the end of the letters and have a more established feel to them. Think of Times New Roman, Garamond, and Bodoni. A lot of high-end fashion brands use serif fonts like Dior, Prada, Versace. Mercedes Benz and TIME magazine also use serif fonts. It gives off a certain timeless feel, which is what these companies are aiming for in their typographic choices.

Sans serif fonts, on the other hand, don't have the little feet at the ends of the letters; instead, they use crisp lines and either sharp or round edges, which make them feel modern and clean. Sans serif fonts are popular with tech companies like Google, Amazon, and Spotify. Popular sans serif fonts are Helvetica, Gill Sans, and Futura.

When choosing typography for your personal or professional brand, which will probably be seen in your social media posts, consider your tone of voice and how you want to visually communicate.

Loud and proud? Consider a bold sans serif font.

Traditional and academic? Consider a serif font.

Graphic designers around the world will cringe when I say this, but check out Canva.com. It's an online DIY design site where you can find not only pre-made templates for social media posts, but you can also select type combinations that are already paired in a way that's good looking and has a designer's eye.

One of the problems using Canva is that if you simply copy/paste a pre-designed template and pop it into your social media, chances are that someone else has the exact same template, and it will not help you stand out. There are designers who can create social media templates and put them into Canva for you to use on your own. I recommend doing this so you'll know that you have your own design and style that matches your personal brand that can't be copied.

Typographic choices are very important because no one reads. Seriously. Start to notice how you scan a newspaper or the headlines on your phone. If you read a headline and it piques your interest, you'll read the sub-head. If you aren't interested, you skip it and move on to the next headline. Differentiating between your headline font and smaller fonts, to support your message, are important to capture your reader's attention.

Size differences in typography:

# HEADLINE = BIGGEST TYPE ON THE PAGE

## Subhead = Supports the Headline

Body Copy = it's only read if you've captured attention using the typography above.

**Photography**

Feeling shy about showing your face online?

"Toughies, kid," as my dad would say.

You are the face and "personal" part of your brand. Photography invites people into a real, or online conversation; this is why dating apps work, and this is why candidates land interviews from LinkedIn. Period, end of story. People want to connect with you. Personal photography of your smiling friendly face is crucial to enhance the know, like, and trust factor.

## MESSAGING AND VISUAL CONTENT

Lifestyle photography captures real-life events in an artistic way, as if you are inviting the viewer into a moment of your day. Long gone are the days of portrait photography, sitting at a ¾ turn towards the camera with perfect JCPenney's lighting. Instead, lifestyle photography captures a burst of laughter, a glance, a hug, or a feeling in everyday moments.

What audience you are trying to attract will determine what photography style you are going to need. If you are building a professional brand because you are a thought leader, author, or executive, you'll need professional photography that is clear, clean, and impressive. Maybe it's you next to a whiteboard doodling a brilliant idea, or at a modern white desk with a co-worker brainstorming on a project together, or giving a talk with a microphone in hand.

If you are building a personal brand that is attracting a twenty-to-thirty-something audience to talk about Gen Z issues, then you'll need photography that reflects what's of the moment and off-the-cuff. Maybe it's on a couch with friends, better yet—outside on a couch, because why not? Playing guitar, next to a fire, in a hammock. Or you on a bike or skateboard heading to work.

One of my favorite photographers in Chicago is Lauren Michelle Clark. She was a client of mine as she transitioned from being a graphic designer at a design studio to a full-time entrepreneur. At least once a year, I put together three outfits, and we walk around the West Loop neighborhood of

Chicago, where she snaps pictures of me for my social media and website.

The West Loop was the meatpacking district before tech companies like Google and Grubhub moved in. There are lots of murals and textured walls of worn graffiti, as well as outdoor cafés and interesting nooks, concrete staircases, and alleyways. Some of my favorite shots are from a shoot in the summer of 2019. I'm next to a blue checkered wall with a red suit on, and the contrasting colors are amazing! I have a red leopard print scarf that I'm tossing up and down like a lasso, and it captured energy, fun, and unexpected movement in the photos. To this day, those are my favorite lifestyle shots because of the stunning and unanticipated energy we created together. Pop over to bebrightlisa.com to see them.

Here are some tips and tricks to use in a lifestyle photoshoot. Depending on your intention for your shoot, pick and choose what works best for you and your photographer.

## WHEN YOU ARE ON LOCATION WITH YOUR PHOTOGRAPHER

### Overdo It, on Purpose

I want you to dress with 150 percent more style than you normally would on a good day. Be tailored and put together with bells and whistles like jewelry, nice shoes, and purses. You are creating an atmosphere of your high-end presence.

## MESSAGING AND VISUAL CONTENT

I try to wear three different outfits and extend each of their looks by using some tricks of the trade:

One top + One bright jacket + One scarf = Three shots

1. with the jacket on
2. with the jacket off (top only)
3. with the jacket and scarf (play with the scarf with your hands)

Wear bigger and bolder jewelry than normal.

Get a manicure.

If you feel comfortable doing your own make-up, cool: but wear 30 percent more makeup, specifically blush which will make you look alive and vibrant on camera. Or, you can always hire a make-up artist. Ask friends who have done photoshoots, or ask a friend who recently got married; they'll know where to find a makeup artist. You can also book an appointment at a makeup counter like Bobbi Brown or MAC at a department store like Nordstrom or Macy's.

## Location and Prop Ideas for a Professional Lifestyle Shoot

Choose a café, co-working space, outdoor sitting area, the lobby of an upscale hotel, a well-lit alleyway, or urban space.

**FIND YOUR CLEAR VISION**

Consider bringing any of these items:

- Purses
- A computer (make sure it's clean and wiped down)
- A notebook or journal to pretend you're taking notes
- A few pens or pencils
- Your phone to pretend to take a call or to check your phone with a smile on
- A reusable coffee mug from home if that's your thing
- A book

## Location and Prop Ideas for a Personal Lifestyle Shoot

Choose an event for a real-life feel, or a party, a playground, or a nature space like a conservatory, forest, or lake.

- Prayer beads
- Meditation or yoga mat
- Guitar, musical instrument, or headphones
- Bubbles
- A glass of wine or water

## MESSAGING AND VISUAL CONTENT

### Pose Ideas

When I owned my design studio, I worked with fashion models on retail shoots, and they were always moving their body weight side to side, using their hips and shoulders to help add dimension to their body, and you can do it too; simply keep moving.

Place your hands on different areas of your body, like your waist. Playing with your hair, a necklace, or a pen will give your hands something to do.

You don't have to look straight into the camera. Look to the side or down; it will give your photography movement and help you avoid looking stiff.

Avoid crossing your arms. It closes off your body rather than making you open.

Sticking your chin out and slightly down will help with any double-chin issues and instantly makes your neck look long, lean, and elegant. It feels ridiculous, but it works. Try it in a mirror.

Avoid putting your hands on your hips—it's the widest part of your body; instead, cup your hand around your waist. It will accentuate your waistline. But if you do, put your hands on your hips, pop your hip to the side, or tilt a shoulder forward to add movement.

**FIND YOUR CLEAR VISION**

Getting your photo taken may feel awkward, and your Ego will pop up with all kinds of excuses about how silly you feel, but do it anyway. Be ridiculous on purpose. Your photographer isn't judging you; they are there to help you look your best. Fifteen minutes of silliness can result in thirty great shots that shine light on your most vibrant self so others will connect with you—and your vision will spread like wildfire.

## Gimmick Limit

The final element to build a personal or professional brand is actually one to not overdo: your gimmick limit.

A gimmick is one detail you use to attract and retain attention. "Be Bright" is my gimmick. The name of my coaching practice is Be Bright Lisa, and I use it as my signature in emails. I wear bright colors and use vibrant juicy watermelon, electric blue, and warm yellows in my social media.

If I posted a photo of me meditating in a grassy field on a dewy morning with an airy script that shared an enlightened Buddha-like quote about peace, it would confuse people. It wouldn't be recognizable as my brand; it's too many gimmicks.

You get one gimmick; that's it—one thing that makes you stand out that's yours, and you own it. Any more and you look silly.

## MESSAGING AND VISUAL CONTENT

### *These Celebrities Use a Gimmick*

- Elton John, the star with flamboyant glasses

- Bruno Mars, the slick performer with silky shirts

- Martha Stewart, anything traditional and slightly frumpy

- Billie Eilish, the rebel with green and black hair

- Jessica Alba, the honest everywoman

- Amelia Dimoldenberg, YouTube interview sensation with Chicken Shop Date (look her up—she's ridiculously funny)

You don't need a gimmick; it's simply another element in your brand to make you stand out and be memorable. If you start to think about it, you probably already have a gimmick...it's something that's repetitive in your life, lifestyle, or closet. Is it your:

Shoe collection?

Purse collection?

Record collection?

Bright pink lipstick?

Love of coffee?

**FIND YOUR CLEAR VISION**

Love of black and white movies?

Pop culture?

Surfing?

The Chicago Bears?

Visual branding is happening all around us. Paying attention to these six elements—tone of voice, your name, typography, photography, color, and gimmick—are an easy way to kick off your visual brand to support your vision.

Sharing yourself with the world in a bigger way can be fun, and it certainly doesn't have to be perfect. Play with it and choose elements that bring a smile to your face and that you are going to enjoy seeing and working with over time. It's not fixed in stone, and you can update as you would update your wardrobe, but do your best to find a brand look and feel that you can maintain consistently across all platforms you are engaging with for at least a year. That will give your audience time to know, like, and trust you.

There you have it. You are someone who is deeply committed to your Inner Platform and self-aware of your Paradox. Your energy is ever-expanding which helps you laser focus on your Visionary Values. You have the tools and strategy to shine. Now is the time to step into your Outer Platform with confidence, conviction, and style.

The world has never been so ready for you.

# CONCLUSION

I REMEMBER PULLING OFF THE HIGHWAY A FEW MILES from my parents' house and onto an empty overpass on New Year's Eve. A deep midnight blue froze the air and my fingertips. I pulled over because I couldn't read the green highway signs. The letters were fuzzy, and light shot out of the left-hand side of my vision. Like a fractured flashlight, the R looked like a D with wings, and the A like an O with a tail. I was blessed to have had 20/20 vision until that day. It was the first time I noticed the scar in my cornea, from Shingles, was blurring my vision.

My identity was tied up in my eyesight because I was a visual graphic designer. I thought, "What am I going to do? Who am I if I can't be a designer?"

I knew I had to reinvent not only my career path but my sense of self, my inner dialogue, and my identity. I needed to find out who I was.

It's been a journey. I'm still driving down the backroads, trying to find my way through new and sometimes rough terrain. It's

## CONCLUSION

not always a clear road sign-off I-70. Sometimes it's a quiet moment on the phone with a loved one telling me that I'll be okay, I've got this. Sometimes it's my spiritual guide or business coach telling me to trust myself, or my kids dropping a brilliant insight, that if I wasn't listening closely enough, I would have missed.

Whatever the path is, it's mine.

You have a path too. You are here, on this planet, at this exact moment in time, for a reason. That alone gives you agency to create your next moment, and the moment after that. Moments become days, weeks, and years. The gift of time is an opportunity to weave together a new pattern of your own. The gift of choice, along with choosing an elevated pop instead of a drop, is an opportunity to change the course of your life. You have agency to choose your Clear Vision every day because this is your one and only life.

Creativity is everywhere, woven into the fabric of your being. It ebbs and flows in your personal and ever-expanding energy. It's ready to burst forth when you call upon it, nurture and care for it. Creativity is your new life partner, your BFF, and your best-kept secret. Trust her. You've got the roadmap to a new path, one of your own invention.

Your path may be cloudy, and sometimes dark, and that's okay. Scary movies don't happen in broad daylight; they happen in the darkest of nights when you feel alone and unsure of

## FIND YOUR CLEAR VISION

yourself. You have a bright inner light—your Inner Platform—which is filled with self-awareness, inner trust, and a clear mindset. And when you are ready, shine your light out so others can see your vibrant Clear Vision.

Share. Embolden us. Brighten our day by being you.

Your clear journey has begun.

I see you becoming more you.

I see your self-awareness blooming like a lotus.

I see you using vulnerability as a clue for curiosity.

I see you leading energy with empathy.

I see you asking and receiving inner guidance.

I see you welcoming wonder—breathing, eating, and dreaming it.

I see you hovering in the unknown with your feet firmly rooted in inner trust and knowing.

I see you overflowing with a stream of ideas, flowing in and out—and yet you,

my friend, are calm in the anarchy of overwhelm.

## CONCLUSION

I see you expanding your capacity to be with more—time swells at the snap of your fingers.

Your curiosity is a superpower.

Your intuition is loud, lively, and secure.

Your Ego is tamed.

Your Vision is a prism of light.

Your spontaneity is electric.

Your imagination is water, soil, and sunshine.

Your energy is your Clear Vision.

You asked me, "Who am I to be this person?"

Friend, your soul has a body and a voice.

See? You just are.

Be bright,

Lisa

# ACKNOWLEDGMENTS

I WANT TO CELEBRATE AND HONOR THE PEOPLE WHO helped me throughout my book journey.

Thank you, Randy. You are my love and my partner. You are my caretaker when I wobble and need someone to lean on. Thank you for taking the muffins to Taekwondo on Saturday mornings so I could write by the big window in our kitchen. I love you to the moon and back.

Thank you, Mom and Dad. Dad, you taught me to love the details of stories and tradition. Mom, you taught me to bring joy and creativity into everyday moments. Without your love, support, and commitment to me as a creative woman, I wouldn't be who I am today. You both believe in me, which is why I believe in myself.

Thank you Sam, Ben, Julien, and Catalina. I am so proud of who you are becoming. You help me laugh and learn more about myself every day.

## ACKNOWLEDGMENTS

Thank you to my brother Lewis and sister Katie. You both are examples of what it means to live a life of integrity and love.

Thank you to my fun-loving, disco-dancing friends. You know who you are—you are wild, spontaneous, and big-hearted. You say "Hell yes, let's do it!" to my crazy ideas and always have my back.

Thank you to everyone who has coached me, listened to me, and held space for my personal growth.

Thank you to my clients who trust me with their stories and transformation. I am honored to be your coach and guide. I wrote this book for you. You are my teacher, as much as I am yours.

Thank you to everyone who contributed their time and energy to the book. Your encouragement, insights, and revisions helped me have the confidence to keep going.

Thank you, Lisa Almquist. You are my spiritual north star and guide throughout the book-writing process.

Thank you, Sylvie Leveiller. You make understanding complex concepts simple through visual design.

Thank you to my editing and publishing team at Scribe Media. From our Tuesday zoom sessions (shout out to my Guided Authors!) to each and every word—you made my book luminous. Thank you Tucker Max, Emily Gindlesparger, Chas

Hoppe, Hussein Al-Baiaty, Darnah Merieca, Nicole Jobe, Janice Bashman, and Jess LaGreca.

Thank you to everyone who read my parts of the book in advance to help me shine: Brian Robinson, Devon Wellman, Danny Evanilla, Andy Crestodina, Marissa Liesenfelt, Madeline Sarad, Andrea Threet, Toni LoCasto, and Stephanie Posey.

Thank you, God, you are my universal bright light.

Made in the USA
Las Vegas, NV
12 April 2023